Crazy But True

Connected to Jesus for Life

Natalie Brand

© Natalie Brand 2014

First published 2014

ISBN: 978-1-78397-066-7

BRYNTIRION PRESS

Evangelical Movement of Wales

The EMW works in both Welsh and English and seeks to help Christians and churches by:
+ running children's camps and family conferences
+ providing theological training and events for ministers
+ running Christian bookshops and a conference centre
+ publishing magazines and books

Bryntirion Press is a ministry of EMW

Past issues of EMW magazines and sermons preached at our conferences are available on our web site: www.emw.org.uk

Published by Bryntirion Press, Office Manager, Evangelical Movement of Wales, Waterton Cross Business Park, South Road, Bridgend, CF31 3UL / Rheolwraig Swyddfa, Mudiad Efengylaidd Cymru, Waterton Cross Business Park, South Road, Pen-y-Bont ar Ogwr, CF31 3UL

Tel/Ffôn: 01656 655886; Website/Gwefan:www.emw.org.uk

In association with EP BOOKS, 6 Silver Court, Welwyn Garden City, AL7 1TS

EP BOOKS are distributed in the USA by:
JPL Fulfillment, 3741 Linden Avenue Southeast, Grand Rapids, MI 49548.
E-mail: sales@jplfulfillment.com; Tel: 877.683.6935

Contents

For my 'Little Women',

Georgiana and Beatrice

1 | Spirituality, Life and Death

THE alarm clock buzzes rudely and you bring your hand down on it a little too hard, letting out a long sigh. It is Monday Morning. You are facing another week. While you battle with your hair, make-up, and tights, all of which conspire against you, you try to think up a national emergency that would sanction a day spent in bed.

Yet soon enough you find yourself sitting in traffic, or at your desk, or standing yet again at the kitchen sink, and last night's sermon comes to mind: You think about the joy of the gospel you tasted, the challenges you felt, and you resolve to have a week really enjoying the Lord. You preach to yourself a little, ask God to help you stay focused, and get on with the day. But as you later snuggle down into your warm bed and reach for your Bible, you have a sudden pang of guilt: You've not had a God-thought all day!

We all struggle at times, wondering whether we truly *know* God. Some days we feel we are thriving in our relationship with him. But on others we are pricked with guilt because we are not yearning for God consistently throughout the week. What can encourage us on these Monday mornings? Or maybe it is the mid-week drag that fills you with discontent? Or the worldly delights of a Friday night out with friends? *What can arm us as we face the diversions, temptations, and trials of the week?* Days when we feel depressed or distracted with the demands of our work or family. Days when our passion for the gospel has dried up in the reality of pleasing the boss, keeping the house clean, fighting intense loneliness, or trying *not* to fight with your husband or teenagers. Nights when we are seduced by materialism, glamour, and a life of pleasure: When suddenly the most important thing to us is, 'how do I look in this dress?', 'how do I compare to the other women in the room?', or 'is he attracted to me?'

Crazy Crazy Spirituality

We are living in a 'spirituality' craze. Many contemporary women seek something 'higher' or 'other' to give them peace and self-fulfilment. Our mothers, daughters, sisters, and friends are turning to new forms of meditation, yoga, or Buddhism. Others look to feminism or 'goddess' spiritualities, homosexuality, or a personal expression of self in transgender. We, as a society, are on a hunt for the 'spiritual' but we are no longer on a hunt for truth. The *X-Files* motif 'The truth is out there' is no longer a concern in the twenty-first century … that is so last century! Yet what we really need is not just some other spirituality but a spirituality based on truth.

Reclaiming the Vintage

As a fan of antiques, I love that it is now super trendy to reclaim vintage furniture with some new fabric and a lick of 'shabby-chic' paint. I always get goose-bumps snooping around antique shops and second-hand emporiums. My heart beats fast with excitement as I turn another corner in anticipation of finding some long lost treasure with its own secrets and stories. Just imagine a gorgeous vintage leather armchair hidden at the back of a dusty antiques emporium, hidden from view under a debris of tasselled cushions and washed-out curtains, waiting to be discovered for the gem that it is.

In all the new ideas on spirituality; the latest Smartphone 'app' or self-help franchise; what we need most is to reclaim a spirituality of truth. This little book is a rediscovery of a spirituality based on the truth of the Bible. Instead of swinging around aimlessly, trying all the different spiritualities and philosophies on offer, in these pages we will anchor spirituality on raw God-truth from God's Word. The Bible is like that vintage armchair; it is a profound treasure that our society has pushed to the backroom. Yet it is beautiful (in a goose-bumps kind of way) and deeply relevant to us women in the twenty-first century. So we will dive head-first (letting our brain do some work and not just our senses) into the theme of being joined to Jesus from the New Testament.

A Wooden Cross For Today

Most of us have heard the Christian saying, 'Jesus died for your sins'. Have you ever wondered what that actually means? How can someone else die for our sins? How can a 2,000 year-old Roman cross in Palestine have any influence or power in our lives today? This book answers these questions.

Jesus of Nazareth ... the man who was pulled down from a brutal Roman cross after being nailed to it, hanging for hours in a state of asphyxiation, and stabbed ... died and was buried in a hole in a rock. Yet three days later he walked out! He died and came back to life. He was buried and raised. The Bible teaches us that if we believe in Jesus we are joined to him; his death becomes *our* death, and his resurrection becomes *our* resurrection. We become women buried and raised in Christ. Without this joining to Jesus the cross of Calvary would just hang suspended in history with no relevance to us at all.

Using This Book

In some chapters of this book we will particularly focus on the New Testament book of Colossians. This is because it is packed full of teaching on being joined to Jesus and how it shapes, not just our spirituality, but our whole lives. Colossians, a letter written to a church formed around the time of 52 AD, confirms that Jesus Christ is all we need in our search for truth. You see, the Christian gospel is not just about how Jesus can save us from our mess but also how he keeps us through all of life. If we are a Christian, he is in us and we are in him and he is *all we need*. This means we can live a life that really enjoys Jesus Christ; he is enough for our Monday mornings, our mid-week drags, and our Friday nights.

As you read this book, I hope you will get a lot out of it. Chapters 2–7 explore what it means to be one with the Lord Jesus and its personal relevance in our lives, while chapters 8 to 10 develop this in our 'community spirituality' in the church. Questions have also been included at the end of the chapters. Whether you are reading on your own, with a friend, or in a group, these can give you an opportunity for personal reflection or stir up further discussion, as well as offer you ideas on acting upon what you have read.

May you catch a vision of King Jesus in this book and grasp more of the crazy truth of being a woman connected to Jesus for life, walking in him every day.

Crazy But True

2 | Jesus is More Than Enough

IN the streets of Brighton the spiritual climate is high. Posters stapled to lamp-posts beckon those who pass by to meet a Psychic, visit a holistic healer, or attend a class in meditation or some other spiritual technique. There is a sense in the city that you can create your own spirituality in the pick 'n' mix offered.

During one short-break in the city, for a treat I booked my first massage. I found myself at a posh self-proclaimed 'urban retreat' called 'Body and Soul'. Inside I was greeted by stone statues from the Far East. Upon entering the dim room that was to be my sanctuary for twenty-five minutes, flickering candles welcomed me as soothing music played and the rich smell of oils filled my nostrils. The whole experience was tailored to promise well-being of mind, body and soul to women ... for a Visa or MasterCard payment. It was a massage for one's aching muscles but I could not help thinking that some women went with an aching soul.

This appetite for 'the spiritual' is not unusual to Brighton. A visit to your local bookshop will confirm the huge variety of products available in the 'Religion' or 'Mind, Body and Soul' sections. Beside books on Islam and Catholicism, you can also buy tarot cards, manuals on finding your 'inner spirit', manuals on finding your 'soul-animal', or your 'inner goddess'. At one large American bookshop I used to frequent you could even acquire a Hindu god with an accompanying textbook or a mini Zen gardening kit. Whatever your spiritual cup of tea, it's out there.

So spirituality has become pretty fashionable in our twenty-first century world. Sadly in all this desire for a personal spirituality that brings peace and happiness, the Christian gospel has been rejected. Today we want connection to a 'Higher Power' without traditions, rules, and responsibilities.

What are we thinking of when we use the term 'spirituality'? Of course, this is a subject under much debate. But here we will simply understand 'spirituality' to be the daily pursuit of the spiritual, that is, the *reaching outside of self for that which is seen to be ultimate*. As Christians, we believe the God of the Bible is THE ultimate being. Therefore, what we need is a spirituality that is solidly biblical and thoroughly reliable.

God's Word

These spiritual trends are confusing for Christian women. We all see what the world has on offer through the media and the latest craze talked, texted, blogged, or 'tweeted' about, but how do we filter these ideas? How do we know what is right and true or unhelpful and incompatible with the gospel? It is essential that we turn to God's Word. Only our Bibles can truly help us.

In their pages the eternal God speaks personally and powerfully to each of us. And in His Fatherly care He gives us answers and direction for the whole of our lives. Remember, as the Bible says of itself, 'All Scripture is breathed out by God and profitable for teaching, for reproof, for correction, and for training in righteousness' (2 Tim. 3:16 [ESV]). As Christian women living in today's world, the Bible is our own God-given resource for spirituality. Our lives should be shaped by it. If we have a spirituality based on something other than the Bible then it is dangerous.

The church in Colossae also struggled with novel ideas on spiritual life buzzing through their ranks. The Apostle Paul wrote to this new Christian community, living in what is now southern Turkey, in the New Testament letter of Colossians. Paul was painfully aware that these Christians lived in a Roman society with a multitude of 'man-made' ideas relating to the divine. Pagan deities and mysterious secret cults were the flavour of the day. Undoubtedly the Colossian Christians were finding it tricky to keep their heads above water and not be pulled under by those who mixed the gospel with other beliefs.

Yet some visitors had made their way into the church family and were disturbing the group with promises of deeper Christian experience and knowledge additional to, but not contradicting, the gospel. These false teachers had come amongst the church family claiming that they knew the secret to a fuller spiritual life. But their 'secrets' had not been part of the gospel that Paul and the Apostles had taught these new Christians. We read one of Paul's warnings regarding this in chapter 2 verse 8. 'See to it that no one takes you captive by philosophy and empty deceit, according to human tradition, according to the elemental spirits of the world, *and not according to Christ.*'

So how does Paul help the Colossians? Simply ... he presents Jesus Christ to them. Instead of teaching some new angle about how to know Jesus more, Paul tells them that as Christians they possess the person of Christ. Christ is their own. The Apostle teaches them that through their faith they enjoy a special unity with him. And because the church is in a saving union with Jesus, they need nothing else! This is their true, authentic spirituality.

Let's look further at what Paul writes to encourage and strengthen the Colossians in the faith and away from the nonsense of these 'theological troublemakers'. Paul knows that the best antidote for this confusion is to give them raw undiluted truth about God. So he makes sure that the Colossians are clear about their glorious Saviour by writing them a letter that revolves around the kingship of Jesus and the fact that he is all they need. This God-inspired book can clear up our confusion too and help us be women who keep our eyes fixed firmly on our Lord and Saviour.

Jesus Our Supreme Saviour

Who is Jesus? 'He is the image of the invisible God' (Col. 1:15). After all the greetings, introductions and prayers (vv.1–14), Paul goes right to it in verse 15. He is the physical representation of God. Our Jesus is fully God. 'For in him all the fullness of God was pleased to dwell' (Col. 1:19). This is staggering. This man who walked the dusty ground of Palestine is a full member of the Godhead!

This section between verses 15 to 20 of Colossians chapter 1 is sometimes understood to be a hymn all about the person of Christ. This is not surprising since in these few verses, the Apostle seems to shout about who Jesus is, his power, his kingship, his deity, his supremacy, as well as what he has done. Paul wants his readers to know that Jesus is King, and because he is God he has no rival.

The God-Man

Throughout Paul also reminds us that our King Jesus shares our humanity. He is the God-Man. Paul writes, he is 'the firstborn of all creation' (v.15). Here Paul is referring to Jesus as the human fulfilment of the small broken body of the lamb whose painted blood saved the life of every Hebrew first-born son on Passover night, during the Israelites' last days in Egypt (Exod. 12). As God's 'first-born' Jesus saves us by his blood, not just for one dark terrible night, but for now and always, even after death.

As God, Jesus was present and active in creating the earth at the beginning. 'For by him all things were created, in heaven and on earth, visible and invisible, whether thrones or dominions or rulers or authorities—all things were created through him and for him' (Col. 1:16). If all things were created 'by', 'through', and 'for' him, then Jesus must have existed before creation. We must not forget that our Saviour lived *before* his Christmas birth on earth as a man. There are many times when Jesus confirms this himself in the New Testament's gospel accounts. This is why he prays in John 17; 'And now, Father, glorify me in your own presence with the glory that I had with you before the world existed' (John 17:5). This is what Paul means when he writes, 'he is *before* all things, and in him all things hold together' (v.17). Every day we take for granted the harmony of our planet. But where would it be without Christ's cosmic power sustaining it?

So Paul is teaching that Jesus is the forerunner and ruler of creation, but he himself was not created. He has always existed. And he is supreme over creation, as the God-Man he stands at the centre of it all. These things are hard for us to grasp. We are talking of eternal God-truth. As human beings, as small and limited as we are, we must recognise the mystery of our God. God would not really be God if we had him completely figured out. This is tricky to get our heads around I know ... but stay with me—these truths can change your life.

The Personal

Paul continues and makes it personal, 'And he is the head of the body, the church' (Col. 1:18). Paul comforts the Colossians with the fact that Jesus is intimately leading and guiding them in their own situation. This is not abstract, but practical and personal. Christ has authority not only as King but also as head. In the same way that the head is vitally connected to the whole body, so Jesus is not distant but united personally to the church. This must have been a great comfort to the Colossians. They were not alone, having to fight for truth in a community beset by troublemakers. The reality of the situation was that their Lord and Saviour was sovereignly leading and guiding them. This is an encouragement for us too. If Jesus is supreme over the church then he is supreme over its disappointments. Christ is bigger than the blows and persecutions that society might deal to the church and its Christian faith.

The Authentic

Because Jesus is supreme over everything, he is the *only* genuine Saviour. He is totally dependable. He is not a god (with accompanying textbook) we can buy from a local bookshop, or a lifeless idol carved out of wood. King Jesus is 'the first and the last' (Rev. 1:17), supreme over the whole of planet earth; over deep space, over the skies and seas.

And Jesus Christ holds us together (Col. 1:17). He is Lord over our DNA, our bone marrow, our cancer, our arthritis, our appearance, our fatigue, our infertility, our anxiety, our depression: Lord over our finances, our singleness, our marriage, our unbelieving spouse, our rebellious children, our loneliness, our losses, our failures, and our successes, our work or our retirement. This means it is the same gentle but powerful pair of hands that formed planets and solar systems that keeps us in one piece, comforting us when we are broken about life.

And these same hands give us victory at the cross. For Jesus is Lord *even* over death; the one power which renders every one of us powerless; 'He is the beginning, *the firstborn from the dead,* that in everything he might be preeminent' (Col. 1:18).

King Jesus trounced death. That fateful curse, which in life haunts us with its finality, was crushed. Which is why Paul writes in 1 Corinthians, 'O death, where is your victory? O death, where is your sting?' (1 Cor. 15:55). If Christ is our own, if we acknowledge him as our authentic Saviour, then death is really no death for us since our last breath is the start of an eternal life with him. Even now he is waiting to take us to his heavenly home to be with him forever (John 14:2–3).

Conclusion

Jesus came with life on his agenda and through the cross he hammered sin and death. What a wonderful truth that as Christians we are spiritually joined to King Jesus whose, 'grace is sufficient' for us and whose, 'power is made perfect in weakness' (2 Cor. 12:9).

You may ask, 'how can I really walk with Jesus in my daily life?' It is through understanding and wielding the truth of our union with him, which is the topic of this book.

Discussion Questions

1. Why are people not interested in Christianity? Think about your non-Christian friends and relatives.

2. How should the fact that Jesus is head over the church encourage us in our church life?

3 | Jesus is Sufficient

HAVING confirmed the superiority of Christ the God-Man and his victory over death, the writer Paul now turns to what Jesus *achieved* through his death: The work 'to reconcile to himself all things, whether on earth or in heaven, making peace by the blood of his cross' (Col. 1:20). Because of who Jesus is, because in his miraculous person both divinity and humanity are supernaturally united; he is our sufficient Saviour. Only the untainted God-Man could take on all the mess of humanity and stamp out sin with his innocent blood. Only the powerful God-Man could reconcile a holy God with rebellious humans. It is because Jesus has the utmost supremacy in all things that his death is more than adequate to do what would be otherwise impossible. That is why Jesus said, 'it is finished' on the cross. The deal is done. Our death penalty has been transferred to him. The bill is paid. Our slavery to sin and death is over because our Saviour is enough. His death and resurrection are powerful enough to rescue us.

So we need nothing outside of Christ to save us. The theological-troublemakers were coaxing the Colossians to extreme spiritual practices, such as fasting and rituals, and warped ideas on the worship of angels and visions. Paul writes, 'Let no one disqualify you, insisting on asceticism and worship of angels, going on in detail about visions, puffed up without reason by his sensuous mind, and not holding fast to the Head' (Col. 2:18–19). Paul calls such ideas 'sensuous'. So although these teachings might sound super-spiritual, Paul writes them off as excessively physical (or carnal), extravagant, and produced by pride. The teacher of these notions is allowing his mind to shape his spiritual life instead of 'holding fast to the Head', who is Jesus Christ. 'These have indeed an appearance of wisdom in promoting self-made religion and asceticism and severity to the body, but they are of no value in stopping the indulgence of the flesh' (Col. 2:23).

Gospel Reality

Christ's sufficiency can become clearer to us when we understand how horrific our sin is and the mess we are. Sometimes we can be so ignorant of how spiritually sick we are that we have no idea we need a doctor as soon as possible. It is only the Holy Spirit who can open our eyes to our fatal condition. Hymn-writer Augustus Toplady knew this when he wrote the line,

'Foul, I to the fountain fly; wash me, Saviour, or I die.'

In seeing how vile we really are, we can do nothing but run as fast as we can to the cleansing fountain that is Christ. This running is not like coming in from a day's country walk, cold and wet and in need of a hot bath. No, it is more akin to the sexual assault victim who rushes to the shower to wash off the offence, the dirt, and the shame. For the reality of the gospel is this: We are all sinners; worthy of nothing but a dark stifling dungeon that reflects our own state. Clinging to our sin we are indifferent to the fact that we sit in our own spiritual filth. And yet God, in his infinite grace, opens a grill in the ceiling, filling the place with light, giving us a first glimpse of our condition. Then, he reaches in and pulls us out, saving us from the grim lifelessness of our situation. But he does not stop there. In the glorious gospel of Jesus Christ, God does not just forgive us. He places us on a palace roof, and clothes us in the royal robes of his Son's righteousness, uniting us to Christ, making us co-heirs with him, and adopting us into His family as daughters of the King. How can such a Saviour be inadequate?

Conclusion

As women in today's world we need a spirituality applicable to all areas of our lives—one that works from Monday to Friday and not just Sundays. This has to be grounded on raw truth, not on fads, experience, or even emotions. Nothing but a spirituality centred on Jesus can genuinely bring redemption, contentment, and wholeness. Otherwise, the core problem of sin is not dealt with and we will continue to stumble around in the dark. Only through King Jesus has the Father 'delivered us from the domain of darkness and transferred us to the kingdom of his beloved Son' (Col. 1:13).

Discussion Questions

1. How can our day-to-day living display the fact that Jesus is more than enough for all of humanity?

2. Pray that God, through his Holy Spirit, would reveal to you your great need of Christ, showing you afresh the glory of the gospel. If you are in a group, pray for one another.

4 | Union with Christ: What is it?

WHEN I went into hospital to have my first baby, I had an experience that demonstrated union with Christ to me in a really vivid way. It was on a morning spent visiting the day assessment unit. We sat waiting for hours in one large room with other patients and staff bustling in and out. I was subject to very brief half-hourly checks. We had to stay in that one room, use one designated 'visitor' toilet, and the only refreshment available to us was water from one of those bubbling dispensers with cone shaped paper cups. Much of the time we were left alone and ignored.

But some time after lunch a doctor visited me and it was finally decided that I would be admitted. In an instant everything changed. Bham! ... A band was smacked onto my wrist and my status radically altered. I was given my own room with my own en-suite; I was entitled to free meals and snacks. I could now venture outside into other areas of the hospital. I had 'buzzer rights' and 24 hour care, and was entitled to receive visitors. In a flash the extortionate bill we had racked up in the car park was waived. I was no longer outside of the hospital. The band on my wrist signified I was part of the hospital and now enjoyed profoundly greater privileges to which I was not previously entitled. My new status of 'admittance' gave me a dramatically different identity and experience.

When a person believes in Christ everything changes in a moment. Bham! … They are 'admitted' into Christ and all God's awesome gifts in redemption are theirs. They are no longer outside of Christ but are part of him; having a new status and identity with new spiritual rights. Now 'every spiritual blessing' and privilege is found *in* Jesus Christ (Eph. 1:3). Privileges such as being uniquely *chosen* by God and *called* to God in Christ, enjoying a first-hand loving relationship with the *whole* Trinity (John 14:23, 26; 1 Cor. 1:9; Eph. 1:4–5; 2 Tim. 1:9): Gifts such as a new supernatural *life* and vitality (Eph. 2:5; Col. 2:13) and eternal *pardon* in Christ (Rom. 8:1; Gal. 2:17; 1 Cor. 1:30). Admittance *into Jesus* means *adoption* into God's intimate family and being a *co-heir* with Christ; entitled to a glorious *inheritance* (Rom. 8:15–17). These children of God receive Holy Spirit power and promise to be *transformed* in Christ, to be *kept* in Christ throughout life, and to *die* in Christ, only to be *raised* when King Jesus returns (Rom. 8:9; 1 Cor. 1:2, 6:11; Phil. 1:6; Rev. 14:13; 1 Cor. 15:22; Rom. 6:5–11; 1 Thess. 4:16–17). None of us can hope to have any of these spiritual joys and rights without Christ and we will unpack some of them in the next few chapters.

This is the Gospel

Once we are united to Jesus we are unbreakably found in him. When we trust in him, everything that belongs to him belongs to us. So behind this little New Testament word 'in' is a crazy reality—a mind boggling truth: Believers are fully wrapped up in their King and Saviour, never to be plucked out.

In all this it is important for us to recognise that union with Christ is not just *central* to the gospel ... it *is* the gospel.

Designed That Way

The question might be asked, 'why did God design oneness with his Son to be the way he saves us?' Well, *union* or *oneness* is at the core of who God is. Do you want to know what the God of the Bible is like? The answer is *Trinity*; Father, Son, and Holy Spirit. Three distinct persons who are one united Godhead, with one divine nature. In the life of the Godhead each person enjoys perfect unadulterated oneness with the other two, there are no favourites. Jesus was speaking of his union with the Father when he said, 'Whoever has seen me has seen the Father ... Believe me that I am in the Father and the Father is in me' (John 14:9, 11).

We cannot understand the nature of the Triune God fully; for God is mysterious and beyond our human understanding. Still we can know that unity, relationship, and loving harmony are on God's agenda. Because of who he is *union* is the way God operates.

Therefore, joining sinners to the eternal God-Man was the life-saving plan from the beginning. '... Even as he chose us *in him* before the foundation of the world' (Eph. 1:4). It was a design born in the Father's infinite love and grace. God the Father 'so loved the world, that he gave his only Son', sending him to earth in human flesh so 'that whoever believes in him should not perish but have eternal life' (John 3:16).

This union design includes all three persons of the Trinity. They all work together to this end. It is the work of the Holy Spirit that powerfully locks Jesus to his church and his church to him. He is the God-bond that fuses those with faith inseparably with their Saviour, and through him, the whole Trinity (Rom. 8:9). This is what it means to be 'hidden with Christ in God' (Col. 3:3). God the Father, God the Son, and God the Holy Spirit are ours because of our new status founded on the wristband of oneness with Jesus.

But how does the Bible describe this union with Christ?

A Vine, A Body, A Couple, And A Building

One way the Bible teaches us about union with Christ is through analogy. We will look briefly at four simple analogies that the Bible draws from four everyday things; a vine, a human body, a married couple, and a building.

Good Wine: A Vine

Fair enough not many of us have a vineyard in our back garden but in Jesus' day and country they would have been a common sight. It is in John 15 that we find Jesus saying, 'I am the true vine', He describes us as branches and God the Father as the vine dresser. 'I am the vine; you are the branches. Whoever abides in me and I in him, he it is that bears much fruit, for apart from me you can do nothing' (John 15:5).

There are many careful specifics in the art of good winemaking. How long a grape is left on the vine, the amount of water the branch consumes, to what degree the fruit is squeezed. The 'terroir' is also important; the soil quality, climate, and the topography of the land. All these factors shape the quality of the wine and its cost. But unless the branches are attached to the vine, the best 'terroir' or the most meticulous controlled watering are utterly pointless. There will be no life let alone fruit or wine! If a branch accidently breaks off the vine, landing on the dusty earth below, it will quickly shrivel up and die. It can do nothing without the vine.

Jesus uses this blunt but obvious life or death fact about the vine to teach us that our union with him is a life or death issue. If we are not united to him we are dead ... dead as a doornail. Jesus says, 'If anyone does not abide in me he is thrown away like a branch and withers; and the branches are gathered, thrown into the fire, and burned' (John 15:6). When we are locked into Jesus by faith he feeds us with his own spiritual life and power; we become spiritually alive. Union with Christ saves us from the spiritual death that we are in without him.

Chosen In Jesus
If we look further at the text we learn more. Jesus goes on telling his disciples that no one can lead a godly life without his life and power. Our spiritual connection to

Jesus puts his life in us so, as Christian women, we are sustained and empowered to be useful and productive for the glory of God. But Jesus also says that it was for this purpose that God *chose* us. 'By this my Father is glorified, that you bear much fruit and so prove to be my disciples ... You did not choose me, but I chose you and appointed you that you should go and bear fruit' (John 15:8, 16).

As well as our faith and life in Christ glorifying God, here the Son of God tells us through his words to his disciples that God the Father chose us *in* him, the God-Man. This means I was not chosen by God as 'Natalie Brand' but as 'Natalie Brand in Jesus Christ', and it is the same for you! *God has only ever thought about saving you and me in Jesus.* This helps us take our minds off ourselves when we think about our salvation and gives us a more realistic, Christ-centred understanding of the gospel. After all, the gospel is from start to finish all about Jesus.

We have seen that the Bible's vine and branches analogy teaches us that our spiritual connection to Jesus puts his life in us. This is a spiritual life that saves us. This life also sustains and empowers us to be useful and productive for the glory of God, bearing the fruit of godliness and an eyes-always-fixed-on-Jesus kind of faith. Such fruit never fails; it is the most excellent wine.

No Headless Corpse: A Body
In our last chapter we read Paul's words to the Colossians, 'And he [Christ] is the head of the body, the church' (Col. 1:18). Paul builds on this in chapter two and we see our

second biblical illustration of union with Christ come to life; that of the human body. He tells them to hold fast to Jesus who is 'the Head, from whom the whole body, nourished and knit together through its joints and ligaments, grows with a growth that is from God' (Col. 2:19).

This picture of King Jesus as the head and the church 'growing up' in him is a favourite of Paul. He does it again in his letter to the Ephesians. 'We are to grow up in every way into him who is the head, into Christ, from whom the whole body, joined and held together by every joint with which it is equipped, when each part is working properly, makes the body grow so that it builds itself up in love' (Eph. 4:15–16. *cf.* 1 Cor. 12:12–31). The church body is alive because it is knitted together to the life-giving head, and because of this it matures and develops as a unit. Like the vine and branches, life and growth are impossible if the head and body are severed.

I see this every day as I watch my two young daughters grow up at sometimes an alarming rate. It always amazes me that everything grows together in unison. Their heads grow together with their sweet frames and each little limb. Even their smaller parts; their hair, ears, and eyes are not left behind. Nothing is out of sync. Their body parts are united thoroughly as they grow, creating uniformity.

It is the same with Christ's church. Bound together by its head, Jesus Christ, the church family grows up into a healthy spiritual body. If the body did not mature in uniformity then some members or parts would be left behind, creating deformity. This is one of the glorious purposes of our union with the Son of God: We are each personally connected to a great Jesus-purchased community that is an intimate part of King Jesus himself. In this community, we mature in our faith and in godliness. And there is more … This body is Jesus Christ's own bride.

Married To The King: A Couple

My favourite description of union with Christ in the Bible is that of the husband and wife. The Apostle Paul draws on this analogy throughout his writing but it is not a new theme. In the Old Testament God is continually described as the faithful lover and husband of his people Israel.[1] Awesome and comforting passages such as Isaiah 54 include mighty yet tender words from God to his people through the prophets: "'For your Maker is your husband, the LORD of hosts is his name; and the Holy One of Israel is your Redeemer … with everlasting love I will have compassion on you,' says the LORD, your Redeemer' (Isa. 54:5, 8).

In his letter to the church in Ephesus, together with his head-body metaphor, Paul draws a powerful parallel between marriage and Christ's intimate union with his church.

Husbands, love your wives, as Christ loved the church and gave himself up for her, that he might sanctify her, having cleansed her by the washing of water with the word, so that he might present the church to himself in splendour, without spot or wrinkle or any such thing, that she might be holy and without blemish. In the same way husbands should love their wives as their own bodies. He who loves his wife loves himself. For no one ever hated his own flesh, but nourishes and cherishes it, just as Christ does the church, because we are members of his body (Eph. 5:25–30).

Marriage echoes the intimacy between Jesus and his church so deeply that Paul even quotes from the book of Genesis.

'Therefore a man shall leave his father and mother and hold fast to his wife, and the two shall become one flesh.' This mystery is profound, and I am saying it refers to Christ and the church (Eph. 5:31–32).

Plain and simple ... Jesus is married to his church. Just as husband and wife become one flesh in marriage, so Jesus is one flesh with those he bought with his blood. Sure, the ever practical Paul is exhorting his readers to godly marriage relationships. He knows marriages of mutual love and respect give glory to God. But he is doing so much more here. *Paul is revealing that human marriage was created by God to reflect the eternal marriage between Christ and his redeemed Bride, the church.* This spiritual, saving union between King Jesus and his church is the prototype or blueprint for the physical, earthly oneness between husband and wife. Jesus Christ is the ultimate Bridegroom who died to save his beloved. His marriage is sealed by his own blood and he can never be separated from his cherished Bride. In this astounding passage the Apostle is stressing that the church is Christ's own flesh. That is why he treasures her, seeking her purity, beauty and good in all he does (v.29).

The similarities between Christ's gospel marriage with his church and human marriage run deep. Just as a bride and groom make a legal promise and 'covenant' to one another, so God does to his people through the body and blood of his Son. There is much that can be said on this biblical teaching and we have only skimmed the surface. Other works, like those given in the 'Recommended Reading' at the back of this book will dig deeper. That said, we must remember that Paul says this marriage is a 'profound mystery' (v.32) and we cannot fully describe such a wonder of God.

Living Stones: A Building

We have seen that Paul uses this head-body image to call attention to the spiritual union that Christians have with each other in their shared union with Christ. This is also true for the last of our four analogies. This is a picture of Jesus as a 'cornerstone' of a great building or temple made up of 'living stones' which are believers (Eph. 2:19–22. cf. Acts 4:11; 1 Pet. 2:4–6). Here we see that God doesn't just unite believers to his Son, he also unites all those he has saved. He wants all his family—as the saying goes—'under one roof', and that 'roof' is Christ.

These teachings should really drive home to us that union with Christ is not firstly something we think of in relation to ourselves as individuals. *Union with Christ is a community truth.* It is about the church, a truly grace-full living building built on Jesus Christ that is cemented together by the power of the Holy Spirit (Eph. 2:22). Don't get me wrong, union with Christ is deeply personal. It impacts us all as Christians in a powerful way. It shapes our time alone with God and who we are. But if we want to understand union with Christ properly we must appreciate that it is most at home in the Bible in a church family context.

Conclusion

Let's summarise briefly what these four biblical pictures have taught us about the oneness we enjoy with our Saviour. The vine/branches and head/body parallels point to the basic fact that our joining to Jesus saves us because we are given his spiritual life. So union with Christ is *spiritual, saving* and *life-giving*. We saw through Jesus' description of a 'fruitful' life that our union with him helps us to live a life that glorifies God by faith and godliness. Our marriage to Jesus *transforms* and '*grows*' us into him, and, just like a human marriage, it contains promises and covenant *faithfulness* and *security*. It is also a 'one-fleshness', so union with Christ is *personal* and *intimate* and we are *chosen* for it by God the Father (theologians call this 'election'). The *mysterious* in-Christ relationship also binds us together with our brothers and sisters in Christ, so it is a *family* or *corporate* union.

So we now have a basic sketch of union with Christ from the Bible. In order to finish it in our next chapter, however, we need to enter a 2000-year-old tomb. The whole reason God unites believers to his Son is to save them. And Christians are saved because Jesus Christ died a painful and humiliating death on a wooden cross.

Discussion Questions

1. Read John 6:35–59. What does this passage teach us about union with Christ?

2. How does the 'community truth' of oneness with Christ change or shape your relationships at church?

5 | Woman Buried, Woman Raised

IN the dim light of the tomb Jesus' skin looked thin and colourless. The two men did not say much to each other as they worked, they were too deeply mourning for conversation. Joseph and Nicodemus carefully wrapped each limb and then the torso with the linen strands, packing the spices in as they went, their busy hands fanning a sweet aroma into the stagnant air of the cave-like tomb. When they reached Jesus' head they were both filled with uncertainty. How wrong it all seemed. How could they bury this man? A man they had both thought to be the Messiah. Nicodemus felt a cloud of sadness surround him as he thought about his dead friend. But remembering time was short and the Sabbath nearing, Joseph continued ... After all, Jesus of Nazareth was dead.

Jesus Buried, Jesus Raised

We can read the Gospel accounts of Jesus' burial in Matthew 27, Mark 15, Luke 23 and John 19. It might have been a grim story; Jesus, an innocent and kind man, the best man ever to have walked the earth, hatefully executed on a Roman cross and hastily buried. Instead of the thud of earth hitting a wooden coffin sitting six-feet under, his burial was sealed by a large rock slowly rolled in front of a small entrance … Never to be opened again.

But the story does not end there. Two sleeps later Peter and John were back in that very tomb, and it was open and empty! Standing where Joseph of Arimathea and Nicodemus had been, Jesus' disciples just stared in surprise, confusion, and hope!

> So Peter went out with the other disciple, and they were going toward the tomb. Both of them were running together, but the other disciple outran Peter and reached the tomb first. And stooping to look in, he saw the linen cloths lying there, but he did not go in. Then Simon Peter came, following him, and went into the tomb. He saw the linen cloths lying there, and the face cloth, which had been on Jesus' head, not lying with the linen cloths but folded up in a place by itself (John 20:3–7).

Jesus had risen!

Jesus Christ was buried and raised and his resurrection is everything to the gospel. If that stone had not been rolled away and the garden tomb remained a place of sorrow instead of a place of Easter celebration, there would be no gospel. It is as we read in 1 Corinthians, 'For if the dead are not raised, not even Christ has been raised. And if Christ has not been raised, your faith is futile and you are still in your sins' (1 Cor. 15:16–17).

The Son of God cannot save us if Jesus is still lying in a sealed tomb in Palestine. Death would have conquered on that day and we would have no Saviour and no hope. But praise God! Jesus did defeat death. The stone was rolled away and the tomb is empty.

Woman Buried, Woman Raised

If you belong to Jesus by believing in him then you too entered that tomb cold and lifeless. And three days later, you also walked out alive and victorious. This is because as women supernaturally tied to King Jesus we were spiritually buried and raised *with* him. This is what Paul means when he writes to the Colossians, 'and you, who were dead in your trespasses and the uncircumcision of your flesh, *God made alive together with him*, having forgiven us all our trespasses' (Col. 2:13). The words 'God made alive together with him' mean that when we are joined to our Saviour we are joined to his death, burial, and resurrection. This is the purpose of our union with him. If we do not share in Christ's death and resurrection how can they have any power or relevance to us?

This death is not the same as the future resurrection of the dead. Of course when Jesus returns he will indeed take all his people back with him, even those who have died, giving us all new heavenly bodies (*cf.* 1 Thess. 4:14–18; 1 Cor. 15:52–57). What I am talking about happens when we become a Christian.

As women buried with Christ we die to a lot of things:

First, we die to our former Christ-less selves, 'Therefore, if anyone is *in Christ*, he is a new creation. *The old has passed away*; behold, *the new has come*' (2 Cor. 5:17). This is why Jesus spoke to Nicodemus about being 'born again' (John 3:3). The new belonging-to-God person that we become when we turn to Christ is transformed by the Spirit of God (John 3:5–6). Although you are the same person with the same personality and body than before, even these things are not the same as they were. Both now belong to God and are prized by him and made holy for his glory (1 Cor. 6:19–20). 'We know that our old self was crucified with him' (Rom. 6:6). The transformation has been immense; we are now joined to Jesus. As we said earlier, I am not 'Natalie Brand' anymore but 'Natalie Brand in Christ' ... I have changed dramatically.

This is closely connected to the next death; we die to the power of sin over us. 'We know that our old self was crucified with him in order that the body of sin might be brought to nothing, so that we would *no longer be enslaved to sin*' (Rom. 6:6). Imagine yourself as a slave in a slave market. Your old boss, Mr Sin, constantly beat you, crushed your joy, and overpowered you at your every word, thought and deed. But as Christ buys you from that tyrant, with his own blood, you are free from that old master. You now have the power to fight sin back, to reclaim your joy, and have holy words, holy thoughts and holy deeds. Sin is no longer your master, Jesus is! All because you were buried and raised with him. 'So you also must consider yourselves *dead to sin* and *alive to God in Christ Jesus*' (Rom. 6:11). As we shall see, this does not mean that we can't sin but that we have the power not to.

This all means we also die to living for self and what the world offers. We now enjoy a new self that is fused to King Jesus, free from sin and death. Building up our own names and kingdoms or revelling in the empty meaningless toys and pursuits of withering-away-planet-Earth just doesn't make sense. Paul agrees, 'But far be it from me to boast except in the cross of our Lord Jesus Christ, by which *the world has been crucified to me, and I to the world*' (Gal. 6:14). Being spiritually buried with Christ results in death to self, sin, and the futility of a fleeting life on a fading sphere; instead we are raised to a new reality where Christ is our life (Col. 3:1–3), and our lives have eternal God-centred purpose.

Baptised Into Jesus

Baptism is a God-given sign of this sharing in Christ's death, burial, and new life. Christian baptism is not a random 'club' initiation to demonstrate that you have joined the Christian scene. It is a physical sign of the spiritual reality that the person lowered and raised out of the water has been admitted into Jesus, and the Holy Spirit has locked them into Jesus' death and resurrection.

We have seen Paul teach this supernatural joining of Christians to Jesus' historical death and resurrection to be the power of the gospel. Otherwise we are outside of Jesus and he can do nothing for us. This is the meaning of the somewhat mystifying Christian saying, 'Jesus died for your sins.' Being fused to Jesus means his death becomes our death, and his resurrection becomes our resurrection.

Paying the Bill

In the next chapters we will begin to see how Paul helps us apply all this crazy God-truth to every area of our lives. Yet before we turn to this, let's have a good hard look at the cross.

As I write I am sitting in the lobby of a hotel ten minutes drive down-hill from my house. The remains of a tall drink of hot chocolate sits on my table. I have not paid for it. I am currently in the debt of the hotel bar. Once I have paid my bill, however, I am no longer in their debt … I am free. On a visit a couple of months ago it was not until the drive home that I remembered I had forgotten to pay. My husband rang as soon as I got home to confess my omission. My outstanding debt was a nagging shackle until I drove down to settle my bill.

The sinful mess we build up in our lives is a painful, suffocating bill we can never repay. As sinful humans, we are in the debt of our holy Creator. We are not free. We try to make resolutions, we say 'sorry' but we continue being unfair, unloving, and selfish. We are racked with guilt and shame only to fail again.

Jesus Christ settled the bill for us when each of his hands and feet were nailed to a wooden beam and he was hung up on a hill to die: 'By cancelling the record of debt that stood against us with its legal demands. This he set aside, nailing it to the cross' (Col. 2:14). Hallelujah! We are free! All our hate, indulgence, lack of self-control, our motorway speeding, our laziness at work, our impatience with our children, sexual sin, impure thought life, our anger, materialism, and rebellion: *All* our sin is nailed to a 2,000 year-old Roman cross! It is no longer ours! This is how the cross of Jesus Christ has power in our lives today.

Conclusion

Many of us are very familiar with Jesus' words, 'I am the way, and the truth, and the life. No one comes to the Father except through me' (John 14:6). I hope that this chapter has made it clear to you that this is more than metaphorical. Jesus is quite literally 'the Way', 'the Truth', and 'the Life'.

We have not covered every aspect of the Bible's teaching on union with Christ. We have only skimmed the surface of this vast and fathomless lake. As we move on, exploring the power that this truth has in our lives, I hope your reading has whetted your appetite and you decide to dive deeper into this truth, in your Bible and other books.

Discussion Questions

1. Have you been baptised as a believer or as a baby belonging to a Christian family? Think back to that special day. In relation to what we have considered in this chapter, do you see it differently now?

2. Think about areas in your life in which you particularly need to know God's grace and forgiveness. Is there a need to talk openly about this with someone else in your group or a friend or family member, asking them to pray for you?

Crazy But True

6 | Woman in the Rock

MANY of us have heard or sung the hymn 'Rock of Ages'. Having cut all my teeth in church, it has long been an overly familiar song conjuring up sepia images of our female ancestors at some old revival meeting, clad in long dresses and hats, belting out, 'Rock of Ages, Cleft for Me, Let me Hide Myself in Thee.' When I was younger I always thought how strange the words were: wondering why we would want to sing about a rock and not really knowing what 'cleft' meant.

What has this centuries old hymn got to do with biblical spirituality for women in the twenty-first century? Well to be honest it was embarrassingly recently that I finally understood what the words meant. One day it suddenly clicked and my first thought was … Moses! There he is in Exodus 33 hiding in a crack in the mountain side. It is important to know that Moses doesn't find the hole and push himself into it. No, God puts him in it because Moses has asked one of the best things we can ask of God. He prays simply, 'show me your glory' (Exod. 33:18).

Moses was asking to see God's power and beauty. For God to reveal who he really is; his attributes, his names, and his

'Godness'. So God graciously hides this tiny little man safely away in a crack in the mountain so that he can truly know the terrifying majesty and awesome power of his Creator.

'I will make all my goodness pass before you and will proclaim before you my name "The LORD." And I will be gracious to whom I will be gracious, and will show mercy on whom I will show mercy …' And the LORD said, 'Behold, there is a place by me where you shall stand on the rock, and while my glory passes by I will put you in a cleft of the rock, and I will cover you with my hand until I have passed by' (Exod. 33:19, 21–22).

As Christian women we are hidden away in the Rock Jesus. This is why Paul writes, 'For you have died, and your life is *hidden with Christ in God*' (Col. 3:3). On the cross Jesus was 'cleft' or broken for us so we could be put graciously 'in' him and be rescued from sin and death by his blood. In the plan of God we are picked up by God the Father and 'concealed', 'wrapped up', or 'sheltered' in Jesus by the Holy Spirit's power. This means we belong to Jesus and Jesus belongs to us, and nothing or no one can change this. We are completely safe and secure from a Godless eternity (a wasted existence spent in filthy sin and judgement) in the rock that is Christ (*cf.* 1 Cor. 10:4).

> *Rock of Ages, cleft for me;*
> *Let me hide myself in Thee;*
> *Let the water and the blood,*
> *From Thy riven [wounded] side which flowed,*

Be of sin the double cure,
Save me from its guilt and power.

A woman buried and raised with Christ is spiritually locked tight into her Saviour. It is a relationship that is secured by Christ's death. When we struggle with broken relationships, or singleness, or the sin of our husbands, we can remind ourselves that we are safe in Christ. He will never leave us or betray us. This Rock doesn't move or disappoint! We can rejoice and find comfort in the fact that we are spiritually married to the faithful King Jesus; the most handsome of the sons of men (Ps. 45:2). He is ours and we are his (Song of Songs 2:16).

Wielding Our Sword

Everything the Bible teaches is there printed in black and white (and red in some Bibles) to be actively applied to our lives. This is why God has given us the Bible, 'All Scripture is breathed out by God and profitable for teaching, for reproof, for correction, and for training in righteousness, that the woman of God may be complete' (2 Tim. 3:16–17). God-truths in the Bible should not be head knowledge alone. As women sheltered in Christ we need to develop the skill of 'wielding' or 'appropriating' gospel truth, like great swords in our hands.

A few months ago some friends of ours had a little baby boy. Because the husband is Scottish, they chose to name their son 'William'. But it was William's middle name that was the real education. 'Claymore' was not a name I knew, and upon asking about it I was told a Claymore was a huge two-handed double-edged sword used by Scottish Highlanders. I immediately had images of Mel Gibson in a kilt, brandishing a long-sword as William Wallace.

In the book of Ephesians, the Bible is described as the 'Sword of the Spirit' (Eph. 6:17), and in Hebrews we read, 'For the word of God is living and active, sharper than any two-edged sword' (Heb. 4:12). The Bible is powerfully relevant and life-changing because it is straight from the mouth of God—it is his Holy and awesome Word. And it is the Holy Spirit who uses it to make us holy, firing it red-hot in our lives.

Perhaps the best thing about a Claymore is its shape. Its handle and blade form a cross. When we wield the Word of God in our lives we are wielding the power of the cross. We are appropriating God's salvation plan in his Son and his victory over Satan at Calvary. Once we appreciate some of the infinite glory of our union with Christ, we can put it to good use: fighting temptation when sin sneaks up with the fact that it was defeated by Jesus' majesty and power. We will consider this again later.

A Biblical Spirituality

Let's get back into Colossians and see how Paul continues to teach his readers about their spirituality and union with Christ. In our previous chapters we saw Paul give a majestic portrait of who Jesus is and the power of his saving work as we are buried and raised with him (Col. 1:15–20; 2:11–15). Now Paul starts applying this more deliberately to the Colossians' lives; opening their eyes to a biblical spirituality centred on Jesus. Paul has reminded his readers of the wonder and might of the God-Man, but now he wants to see them take action and responsibility; to practically live out their bond with him.

In chapter 2 Paul urges, 'Therefore, as you received Christ Jesus the Lord, *so walk in him, rooted and built up in him and established in the faith*' (Col. 2:6–7). In other words, 'you spiritually belong to Christ and he belongs to you, now let it change your life.' There is a lot in these two verses for us in contemporary life. Here Paul gives us a simple yet clear vision of a spirituality based on truth. This spirituality might be summed up as 'walking in Jesus'. Not 'walking *with* Jesus', our great spiritual connection with him makes it much more than that. We walk *in* him.

In this Colossians 2:6–7 vision we can see a woman who journeys through life enjoying her spiritual life 'in-Christ'. The foundations of her life are deeply grounded in Jesus (for she is 'rooted' in him (v.7)) and this produces in her a strong, firm, and mature faith (as she is 'built up in him and established in the faith' (v.7)). But what does it mean to have your foundations rooted in Jesus? And how can we be built up in Christ?

What is more foundational to women than our homes, our identities, our relationships, our womanhood, and how we deal with pain? In the next chapter we will take a fresh look at these major areas in our lives with our 'one with Christ' worldview, and so begin to understand how we can grow up and mature in Jesus.

Conclusion

The glory of being 'in-Christ' offers a far more encouraging view of the spiritual life than many of us actually have. Some of us think of our relationship with God as dependent on our 'quiet times'. If we don't spend time doing spiritual things like reading the Bible or Christian books and praying we are not spiritual and not walking with God. Yet union with Christ blows this unhealthy mindset out of the water! When we are joined to Christ by his Holy Spirit we are *permanently* intersected with God. Although Bible reading and prayer are crucial to knowing God they are not the source of it. Jesus is the source and we are in union with him. This is a reliable God-truth and we can anchor the whole of our lives on it.

Discussion Questions

1. Why is the Bible the best resource for our spiritual lives? Look at 2 Tim. 3:16–17 again.

2. How does your union with Christ, if you are a Christian, shape your spiritual life? Try writing down some ideas.

7 | Union with Christ on Monday Morning

UNION with Christ is a glorious truth. Why is it glorious? ... Because it is endlessly relevant to us and the lives we live. It is not a truth to be locked away in a box in some library. It is to be lived! No matter where we are or what we are doing. Being permanently joined to King Jesus is a remarkable fact that changes everything; how we do our shopping, how we drive, and how we pay our taxes. Being a woman buried and raised with Christ informs our relationships, our decisions, our aspirations, our work, and our leisure. Once we lived only for ourselves but now even the mundane and the trivial are for Christ and his glory!

In this chapter we are going to take the truths that we have looked at since we started and put them into our everyday lives. This will make union with Christ shine even brighter as we see its deep relevance and value, encouraging us to think about how our connection with Jesus affects our Monday to Friday. Still looking at Paul's teaching on the Christian life from Colossians, we will see how our spiritual oneness with Jesus Christ impacts our:

> homes
> identities
> relationships
> womanhood (specifically our sexuality)
> suffering

I encourage you throughout this chapter to think prayerfully and creatively about yourself and your own life, working out how this personally relates to you.

Our Home Sweet Home

A little green cushion sits displayed on our piano's music stand embroidered with the words, 'Home is where the Heart is'. It was a gift from a friend and fits my colour scheme perfectly. Women particularly have their hearts set on their homes. Many of us spend lots of time, money, and elbow-grease keeping our homes clean, beautiful and cosy. In chapter 3 of Colossians, Paul stresses that one practical consequence of being buried and raised with Christ is a shift in where our hearts and homes are. 'If then you have been raised with Christ, *seek the things that are above, where Christ is*, seated at the right hand of God' (Col. 3:1). This is so important that Paul repeats himself immediately in the next verse, 'set *your minds on things that are above*, not on things that are on earth' (v.2). Why? 'For you have *died*, and *your life is hidden with Christ in God*' (v.3). As women buried and raised with Christ we need to look up more.

Earth is no longer home. Our hearts are with our Saviour and our home is where he is.

'Seeking' and setting our 'minds on things above' is pretty counter-cultural with all the emphasis nowadays on the perfect home. Because much of my day involves wiping surfaces, scrubbing kitchen floors, and hoovering bits from the carpet, it is real challenge to focus my thoughts on my true eternal home. Some days, when I find myself dreaming of freshly decorated walls, deep carpets, and elegant buttoned-backed settees, I have to check my heart. Of course it isn't wrong to cherish our homes; they are a great gift from God, useful for his glory. But not one of the pristine homes you find in the home magazines is as stunning as the person of Christ, and our roots are not in bricks and mortar but with him in glory.

Our Facts & Figures

Does it sometimes feel as if you are constantly filling out forms, whether on paper or online? Question after question is posed to us in order to build up our identity. Name? Date of birth? Gender? Ethnicity? Address? Occupation? And occasionally we have to give long accounts of our history; whether medical, educational, family or financial.

Because of this we may ask ourselves, 'how do I look on paper?' We may pride ourselves on our paperwork appearance; our numerous qualifications, an impeccable work history, or an address in a desirable neighbourhood. On the other hand, maybe you shudder at the thought of giving a personal history and are not very impressed with yourself?

A Dodgy Self-Portrait?

Our mirror appearance is similar. As women we allow ourselves to tirelessly engage in constant competition with other women; whether at the shopping centre, the gym, the university library, or the school gate. We compare our hair, our figures, our clothes, and even how our children look. We do it without thinking. It becomes the way we operate.

Each of us has a self-image built up on our paperwork and mirror appearances. This shapes how we relate to ourselves, our friends, our husbands (if we are married), and our Creator. The thing about this self-image is that it is rarely an accurate 'Creator-glorifying' self-portrait. We can easily make too much of it and give it too much power; leading to mood swings, eating disorders, a habitual need for retail therapy, self-harm, and tension in marriage.

Being a woman grounded in Christ is to let our gospel 'in-Christ' status be our first identity. All our identity and self-image stuff is turned on its head when we become a Christian. Our paperwork 'facts' and mirror 'figures' slide away under our new 'hidden with Christ in God' identity. Before we are a mother of three, a civil engineer, an English teacher, a pensioner, a dyslexic, single, or a widow, we are in Christ. Our eternal label as a 'woman in the Rock' far outshines our bulimia, our mental illness, our four or five or even six-figure income, our struggle with homosexuality, or our divorced parents. Being intimately fused to the supreme and sovereign Son of God shapes everything—we only have to let it.

So I challenge you; instead of succumbing to the flood of self-hate that looks to drown women standing in front of changing room mirrors; or before you yield to the 'green-eyed monster' who rears his ugly head in the presence of someone impressive, ask yourself, '*how does my view of myself change because of my identity in Christ?*' '*Can I forego my need to compete with this person because of my perfect acceptance in Christ?*' As women buried and raised with Christ we need to preach to ourselves: 'I have been crucified with Christ. *It is no longer I who live, but Christ who lives in me*' (Gal. 2:20). My identity is in King Jesus.

Our Womanhood

This leads us helpfully into the subject of our womanhood. 'Womanhood' has become a popular topic of discussion since feminism's 'second wave' washed up on our shore in the 1960s. As a result, the sexual revolution with all its baggage of contraception, abortion, and loveless sex have brought chaos to those of us living in its wake. Our culture now seems to predominately define womanhood in terms of sexual expression and freedom. Instead of celebrating God-given differences between men and women, contemporary society prizes a womanhood that demands a 'career with no sacrifices', 'relationships with no marriage', and 'sex with no babies'. This is pretty confusing stuff for us all.

I am grateful that the Bible offers us gritty and honest guidance in the area of sexuality. Of course, since it was written not much has changed; humanity still struggles with the same old sins. Once Paul has reminded the Colossians that Christ is the Christian's life and eternal home (Col. 3:1–4), he goes straight for the throat of our love for sin. 'Put to death therefore what is earthly in you: sexual immorality, impurity, passion, evil desire and covetousness, which is idolatry' (Col. 3:5). You can tell from Paul's list that he is very aware of sexual sin in all its variety. 'Sexual immorality', 'impurity', and 'passion' includes; sex before marriage, adultery, lust towards men or women, venting one's curiosity with porn or masturbation, an x-rated thought life, being sexually provocative, and fooling around with someone in a way that brings guilt the next morning. And Paul says, because we are 'hidden with Christ', put these things 'to death' (v.5). There he goes again with his life and death lingo. Paul does not mince his words. 'Put to death' means 'kill it!' or 'crucify it!'—in the same way that the Romans killed Jesus, who has forgiven you—'flog sin until it dies, because Jesus died for you.'

Saving Our Sexuality

So what do you do when you are asked out by a guy who you know is not a Christian? Or how do you fight the temptation to get carried away with your fiancé because the wedding is only a couple of months away? Or how can you knock the habit of indulging in ungodly fantasies in a lonely single life?

As we mentioned before, our spiritual oneness with Jesus means our female bodies belong to him and are for his glory. 'The body is not meant for sexual immorality, but for the Lord, and the Lord for the body' (1 Cor. 6:13). The Bible says that when we engage in sexual sin, because we are joined to Jesus, we bring *him* into the equation. What a horrid thought!

Do you not know that your bodies are members of Christ? Shall I then take the members of Christ and make them members of a prostitute? Never! Or do you not know that he who is joined to a prostitute becomes one body with her? For, as it is written, 'The two will become one flesh.' *But he who is joined to the Lord becomes one spirit with him* (1 Cor. 6:15–17).

This is not only applicable to men but to women also. If we sin sexually we are bringing the holy and pure Son of God into that situation. Of course, our union with Christ is not a *physical* union, like sex is, but the reality is that the *whole* Christian is joined to Christ. Our souls are not bought by Christ's blood only to leave our bodies with Satan. As preacher Edward Donnelly writes; union with Christ is 'so all-embracing that it includes our physical flesh.'[1]

One thing is important to note as we highlight these sexual sins. Paul's use of the word 'passion' in Colossians 3 verse 5 does not mean that yearning for your husband or wife is sinful. The covenant of marriage is the God-given context for the sex-drive and this brings much glory to God (Gen 2:24; 1 Cor. 6:20; 7:2–5). So we *can* glorify God in our female sexuality. This is good news in all the mess of today's celebrated female promiscuity.

Talking And Walking Away

So how do we wield our union with Christ in the face of sexual temptation? Looking at the beauty of the Lord Jesus Christ is vital; in all his sovereignty and majesty. Our wise old friend Caroline Maria Noel tells us in one of her hymns, written centuries ago, 'Crown Him as your captain in temptation's hour'. We need to talk to ourselves ... *Because I am in Christ and he is in me I will not entertain these impure thoughts ... Knowing that Christ is in me I cannot allow myself to do this ungodly thing with my body.* Try quoting Galatians 5:24, 'those who belong to Christ Jesus have crucified the flesh with its passions and desires' and stomp away victorious, naming yourself a woman connected to Christ, fighting sin with the Holy Spirit's help.

Our Relationships

People can really rub us up the wrong way, can't they? The Bible knows that even the best human relationships are hard. Living as close as we do to family members can particularly be a test of our self-control, Christ-likeness, and graciousness. But an authentic spirituality is not about sitting cross-legged in a field and feeling 'one' with nature. Surely a truly life-changing spiritual life should transform our relationships? One aspect of our maturity 'in-Christ' means learning not to fly off the handle when a household job is not done properly, or forgiving quickly after a harsh or snappy word, or putting others first although we have been let down.

Paul continues to call us to godly living because we are 'hidden with Christ in God' (Col. 3:3). He urges us to 'put away' 'anger, wrath, malice, slander, and obscene talk' from our mouths (Col. 3:8). Paul especially wants us to apply our new 'in-Christ' status to our relationships in our church families. This is why he tells the Colossians not to lie to each other (v.9) and to 'put on love' (v.14), because they have 'put off the old self with its practices and have put on the new self' (Col. 3:9–10). This 'putting off' and 'putting on' is another way Paul expresses our changed life in Christ. It is as though we take off our sin and Christless identity and dress ourselves with Jesus Christ. What wonderful clothes! This is the call to 'put on the Lord Jesus Christ, and make no provision for the flesh' (Rom. 13:14).

Wielding Grace

So Paul tells the Colossians what to take off in their relationships, and now he tells us what to put on: 'Put on then, as God's chosen ones, holy and beloved, compassionate hearts, kindness, humility, meekness, and patience, bearing with one another and, if one has a complaint against another, forgiving each other; as the Lord has forgiven you, so you also must forgive' (Col. 3:12–13).

The powerful thing about these verses are their reference to the gospel. Paul does not say, 'be kind and forgiving because it is good and moral.' He says, 'as the Lord has forgiven you, so you must also forgive.' Because Jesus hung humiliated on a cross to forgive us, we should be quick and generous to forgive others. I have found thinking about Jesus bleeding on the cross during an argument humbles me pretty quickly. Wielding gospel grace to others reminds us that God is constantly forbearing with us through Jesus. Because his awesome grace is sufficient for us (2 Cor. 12:9) we can bend it horizontally to others.

When we clash with our husbands, our parents, our children, or other church members, we can remind ourselves that we don't actually deserve these close relationships that we enjoy every day. Our marriages, our children, our church families—they are all gifts bought by Christ, given to us because of our union with him.

Our Pain

Yet what good is union with Christ when we hand over our child to the surgeons? Or hear the word 'terminal' from across the GP's desk? Or sit in a solicitor's office facing the end of our marriage because of our husband's infidelity? How can union with Christ be appropriated in times of suffering; when deep pain stirs up questions, doubts, and perhaps a crisis of faith?

We all know there are times when life seems impossible. Maybe you endure the daily pain of illness, depression, divorce, bereavement, the backsliding of a teenager, an unconverted husband, or chronic loneliness; feeling the darkness will never lift. Our life-giving union with Christ is really our only source of comfort and security. We might ask, with the Apostle Paul, 'who shall separate us from the love of Christ? Shall tribulation, or distress, or persecution, or famine, or nakedness, or danger, or sword?' (Rom. 8:35). Shall the pain of infertility, or the failure of our exams, or the rejection of our friends? 'No, in all these things we are more than conquerors through him who loved us. For I am sure that neither death nor life, nor angels nor rulers, nor things present nor things to come, nor powers, nor height nor depth, *nor anything else in all creation, will be able to separate us from the love of God in Christ Jesus our Lord*' (Rom. 8:37–39).

We are 'women in the Rock', 'hidden with Christ in God'. When life feels as if it is melting away and we have no control over any of it, here is one certainty that will never change. It is this certainty that can get us through the seemingly impossible. We are kept through every pain by the tenderness of our spiritual husband, Jesus Christ; who himself knew great physical pain, rejection, misunderstanding, and loneliness. We are sheltered in the Son of God who has been through it all.

Bottling It Up

Because of our oneness with his Son, when we suffer God the Father sees it all. And he doesn't just watch from afar, he is actively involved. 'You have kept count of my tossings; put my tears in your bottle. Are they not in your book?' (Ps. 56:8). Here the Psalmist gives us such a beautiful picture of God's care for us even if we despair under the most excruciating pain. Our God fathers us so tenderly even to the point of collecting our tears in his bottle. He is deeply concerned.

A Natural Ingredient

Online blogs and magazines tell us that meditation, positive thinking, breathing techniques, and green tea are all effective for 'spiritual health' and making us spiritually stronger. In our busy and demanding lives, women want to be content and feel strong, especially in times of trial and difficulty.

You may wonder how Paul finishes his letter to the Colossians. In all his teaching and encouragement, Paul finishes by driving home one important aspect of the spiritual life; thankfulness. He writes, 'and let the peace of Christ rule in your hearts, to which indeed you were called in one body. And be *thankful*' (Col. 3:15). In verse 16, Paul charges the Colossians to sing gospel truth to each other 'with *thankfulness* in your hearts to God' (Col. 3:16). And again in the next verse, 'and whatever you do, in word or deed, do everything in the name of the Lord Jesus, *giving thanks* to God the Father through him' (v.17). And lastly in chapter 4, Paul encourages, 'Continue steadfastly in prayer, being watchful in it with *thanksgiving*' (Col. 4:2).

Even though God allows us to go through trials, he is a *good* God and he *does* good (Ps. 119:68). Every trial is given to us in his fatherly love. If God is good and gives us good gifts then it is natural that we give thanks to him. When we are struggling through the day and a smile or a laugh seems worlds away, we can focus on all the 'spiritual blessings' given to us in Christ Jesus (Eph. 1:3), including his use of our suffering to make us holy. James writes, 'count it all joy, my sisters, when you meet trials of various kinds, for you know that the testing of your faith produces steadfastness' (Jas 1:2–3).

Our God doesn't leave us to our pain but counts our tears whilst making us beautiful like his Son. '*Give thanks to the* LORD, *for he is good* ... his steadfast love endures forever' (Ps. 107:1). Recognising God's goodness to us in thankfulness gives us the stamina to get through the tough times.

Conclusion

Truly grasping the force of our union with Christ means we can make it our worldview for life. Like a gospel 'cornea', it can become the lens through which we see everything. This can transform every day of the week.

Discussion Questions

1. Look again at Colossians 3:8–17. What are the key things Paul is teaching in this passage?

2. What can you give thanks to God for today? You could write a prayer of thanksgiving.

Crazy But True

8 | Loving the Bride

KATE and Mark slipped into two spare seats at the back of the church. Kate looked around the large city-based congregation and felt butterflies stir in her stomach. Mark sat slouched as he always did and obviously felt at ease.

She stared at her new husband of just five months and thought, *'it's easy for you. You've lived in London for seven years and moved around in true bachelor style. I've just left my home town with all my friends and family, to be with you ...'* Swallowing hard and self-consciously pulling her cardigan round her stomach to hide her growing bump, Kate looked around for a friendly face. But the other women her age were busy laughing and chatting with each other, oblivious of her. She noticed a woman in her early forties joining her husband in the seat in front. She longed for a reassuring smile.

'Will I ever feel at home here? Will I ever make good friends like back home?' Kate looked at her husband again. *'Will Mark make a good husband and father?'* She wondered glumly.

They had planned to wait a good few years before having children so she could concentrate on getting a graduate position and they could settle into married life. But three months after their honeymoon they had a surprise. '*Lord*', Kate prayed in her head, '*... this wasn't the way it was supposed to be.*' Tears started to sting her eyes, and she suddenly longed for her mum. She wanted a hug from someone other than her husband. Someone to tell her she was not alone. Someone to tell her it was going to be alright. But instead the music started and everyone quickly rose to their feet, leaving her fumbling for the strength to stand. Shaken from her immense feelings of loneliness, the wall of backs now enclosing her was the last straw. With tears streaming down her face, Kate ran from her seat to the refuge all women know best ... the Ladies toilets.

What Women Want

Social academics are telling us that one distinguishing mark of today's woman is her longing for strong connections with other women. We all need good female friends, don't we? When I first got married I really missed my girly bedtime chats with my housemates; sitting cross-legged on one of our beds, sipping a hot drink in our pyjamas and talking about the things that really mattered to us. We women all crave community and camaraderie with others who share our womanhood.

Although our society is still largely individualistic, many contemporary women have become disillusioned with the independent attitude of previous generations. A common thread in many new non-Christian books on spirituality for women (from those within feminist, 'goddess', and Wicca thought) is an emphasis on 'interconnectedness' with others. Today's woman is hungry for relationships that restore and uphold her. Unfortunately some look to loveless sex for this or get hooked onto the endless cycle of failed relationships. Others turn to homosexual relationships with other women.

Women in the church are no different. Many of us reading Kate's story above will be able to relate to it in one way or another. We may be in a different life situation or season from Kate. We may be single or widowed; a student or retired. Yet whether we are in our twenties, thirties, forties, fifties, or sixties; whether we know the uncertainty and isolation Kate felt or we are confident and out-going, embracing life to the full ... we *all* need meaningful relationships with other Christian women. Why? Because we are not alone in our journey of biblical womanhood and sharing the path with others who have been treading it a little longer than us does us a world of good.

Friendships That Glorify God

It may surprise you that the Bible strongly encourages (even commands) meaningful woman-to-woman friendships, even giving details of what they should be like. They are to be friendships that offer advice and support in practical *and* spiritual matters: Friendships marked by openness and honesty, speaking the truth in love: Friendships that have accountability, prayer, and encouragement in holiness at their core, as well as giving a big hug when one is desperately needed.

We may ask why the Bible bothers about these friendships? The answer is that these unique friendships give glory to God.

One in Christ

Before we delve into Titus 2 it is important that we understand the unity that we enjoy with other Christians because of our union with Christ. At the centre of the gospel of Jesus Christ is membership into a family that transforms all who are a part of it. This family or community is not perfect, because it is made up of sinful broken people. But it is a family unlike any other found on earth because it operates on the grace and love of the gospel. It is a 'Calvary community' that gets its identity from the cross of Christ.

As we have seen from Colossians, Jesus Christ is the head of the church (Col. 1:18). All the members of this gospel family are uniquely tied to each other in a spiritual oneness that stems from their leader (1 Cor. 12:12, Eph. 4:3–6, 15–16, Col. 2:19). Because we are each 'wrapped up' or 'hidden in Christ' we are privileged to enter into binding membership to a unique and wonderful community of all those who are united to Jesus. Our oneness with Jesus gives us an oneness with all our fellow brothers and sisters in Christ.

Do you want to walk with Christ in a way that impacts your day to day life? Do you want to really 'taste' the spiritual reality of your union with Christ? What we are going to look at in this chapter is the wonderful truth that one way we can tangibly savour our union with Christ is by actively committing to and enjoying our local church community.

What Is So Special About The Church?
'Oh, no!' You may exclaim. 'Not more about how I *need* to go to church!'

Some of us may have experienced past hurts and disappointments in church life that make us avoid the church like the plague. Perhaps others of us don't really get what the church is for or what it is about. We'd rather sleep in on Sundays, catch up with the housework, or do what our non-Christian friends are doing. If this describes you then you need *God's vision* for church. When it comes to understanding what is so special about the church we first of all need to ask, what does God see when he sees the church?

The New Testament tells us that when Christ looks upon the church he sees his beautiful bride dressed in white, looking radiant. He is choked up with emotion and his heart burns with passion for her because she is *his*. As we looked at in chapter three, the gospel teaches us that Jesus is like a heavenly bridegroom who has bought his bride the church with his precious and powerful blood by his death on the cross. As the head of the church, Jesus cherishes and loves her as a husband.

> Husbands, love your wives, as Christ loved the church and gave himself up for her, that he might sanctify her, having cleansed her by the washing of water with the word, so that he might present the church to himself in splendour, without spot or wrinkle or any such thing, that she might be holy and without blemish ... 'Therefore a man shall leave his father and mother and hold fast to his wife, and the two shall become one flesh.' *This mystery is profound, and I am saying it refers to Christ and the church* (Eph. 5:25–27, 31–32).

So what is so special about the church? Jesus is married to the church.

Loving the Church

This is a challenge to us. As those intimately and eternally joined to Jesus, wanting to live for him and his glory, of course we need to intimately cherish his church. If we are in love with Jesus we must be in love with his bride as well and show this love whole-heartedly, practically and self-sacrificially.

Yet many of us in the twenty-first century have a consumer mentality when we go to church. First, we 'go' … in the same way that we 'go' shopping, when in fact church is more about *belonging* … like a family. You don't 'go' to your family do you? You are part of *it* and *it* is part of you.

We may approach church in an attitude of, 'what can I get out of it?', as if we were watching a film or attending a concert. But church is not a by-product of the gospel. It is not a Christian club that we join because we have become a Christian. No, Church *is* the gospel, because being a member of God's community is a privilege bought by our beloved Saviour. Once we have got a handle on the reality of our union with Christ we cannot continue with these unbiblical ideas of the church. Our local church is our spiritual family. Church life is about commitment, sharing, service, nurture, and unconditional love, not about shopping for something that passively feeds us.

It is as we commit to the life and growth of Christ's body and bride that we can start to exercise our oneness with Christ in a way that spiritually feeds us and others.

Joshua Harris writes in his little gem of a book, *Stop Dating The Church: Fall in Love with the Family of God*, 'Every Christian is called to be passionately committed to a specific local church. Why? Because the local church is the key to spiritual health and growth for a Christian. And because as the visible "body of Christ" in the world, the local church is central to God's plan for every generation.'[1]

Notice not one of the folk in the New Testament restarted life as a hermit in a shack built for one after they had become a Christian. They all got stuck into the messy and sometimes chaotic life of the church, and they all grew in godliness because of this. As Harris challenges us, 'Join a local church and lay down your selfish desires by considering others more important than yourself. Humble yourself and acknowledge that you need other Christians. Invite them into your life. Stop complaining about what's wrong with the church, and become part of a solution.'[2]

Discussion Questions

1. Share openly with the group any way your concept of church has been challenged.

2. Read 1 Corinthians 12:12–31. Why is it so important that members of the church care for one another spiritually, as well as practically?

Crazy But True

9 | The Titus 2 Mandate

AFTER twenty minutes of calming herself in the solitude of a cubicle, Kate returned to her seat with her mascara intact. She avoided Mark's gaze as she fished out her Bible and made herself comfortable as the sermon began. Yet uncertainty continued to nag her, making it difficult to listen to the preacher. As the service drew to an end Kate was in a hurry to make a quick exit. As she got up the lady she had noticed at the start turned around and asked whether they were new or visiting. Surprised, Kate said they had just moved to the area a couple of weeks ago. She noticed the woman's warm expression and felt herself drop back into her chair with a smile. After some exchange about Kate's job-hunting, three small children noisily bounced up interrupting their conversation. A mixture of 'Mum, can you hold my Bible?', 'look at my drawings, Mummy', and 'can I play with Jeanie in the hall?' filled the air and laughter broke across the two women's faces. The lady's name was Rachel and she introduced Kate to her children with admirable consideration and care. Kate liked her instantly.

'So whereabouts are you two living?' Rachel asked.

'Victoria Road,' Kate replied.

'That road is parallel with ours. Do you know the little Deli on the crossroads?'

Kate nodded.

'If you are free and fancy it, let's meet for lunch there this week.'

Joy melted all the tension and confusion of earlier as she and Mark walked to the car later. Kate smiled to herself, honoured that this older woman would show so much interest in her. The anticipation and excitement of her new friend put a spring in her step and she prayed a quick 'thank you' under her breath.

That Sunday Kate knew little of the significance that her friendship with Rachel would have in the coming years of her life. Rachel was to be a great provision from God, giving Kate godly counsel in the early years of her marriage, practical help and support with her new baby, and a means of introduction to the other women in the church. Rachel invested time and prayer for Kate's spiritual life, in turn encouraging Kate to reach out to some of the teenage girls in the church. All these factors pushed Kate to grow up 'in Christ' and thrive in her spiritual, family, and church life.

But what about Rachel? Well, Rachel was not a particularly extraordinary person. But she *was* a woman united to Christ, who as a middle-aged wife, mother and church member, looked to serve God and her sisters in Christ.

This is Titus 2 at work.

Titus Who?

In the book of Titus Paul is writing to a young pastor-in-training who is stationed on the sunny Greek Island of Crete. Titus is a short practical letter about 'faith and practice', demonstrating Paul's pastoral heart for the new Christians there. At this time Crete is an island of self-indulgence and immorality, and because of this, young Pastor Titus is told to be firm with the Cretans for the sake of their holiness (Titus 1:13).

In chapter 2 verses 3 to 5, Paul charges Titus to teach and encourage the older women to care for and disciple the younger Christian women. Paul does not send Titus to teach and disciple the young women himself since this might lead to sexual temptation in opening himself up to inappropriate relationships. The older women are to do the job. Care for the women in the church is important to Paul and he knows men cannot train young women to be godly wives, mothers and homemakers in the same way as their older contemporaries. Paul wants to see the body of Christ actively nourishing and feeding itself.

Have a read of Titus 2. It is a precious guide for each church family to live out their faith by healthy community living. It is an exciting and life-changing text. But more specifically for us women, it is a powerful tool and model for us to employ in our pursuit of biblical womanhood.

Teach And Train

Older women likewise are to be reverent in behaviour, not slanderers or slaves to much wine. They are to teach what is good, and so train the young women to love their husbands and children, to be self-controlled, pure, working at home, kind, and submissive to their own husbands, that the word of God may not be reviled (Titus 2:3–5).

First Paul speaks to Titus of the older men and then, in verse 3, of the older women. It seems Cretan women had a love for their equivalent of Merlot, Chardonnay, or Shiraz. And as we know wine loosens the tongue, the good chin-wags these women enjoyed between sips were known to commonly turn to gossip and slander. So Paul says these Christian women need to be sober and sober-*minded*, behaving in a way that acknowledges God (v.3). And instead of idly sitting around their Mediterranean villas, Paul commissions them to take active care of their younger sisters in Christ. The holiness of these older women is then intertwined with the holiness of the younger. They are to take responsibility and be useful by word and example. This will strengthen their spirituality and help them grow up in Christ.

Biblical Womanhood In Titus 2
In the text Paul is particularly addressing the older women to care for the younger ones who are married and who may or may not have children. The list of concerns are largely practical and domestic; loving and submitting to one's husband, loving one's children, working hard at home, and being self-controlled, kind (or hospitable), and pure in these contexts. Paul is concerned for the women who have families to glorify God by self-sacrificially being hard-working

at home and being good stewards of what God has given them. Not following the current example from their elders of laziness and idle visits for chatter and winebibbing.

But the text is not being exclusive. The description of biblical womanhood in these three verses is a great treasure for *all* Christian women. We don't have the space to look at each in detail but the qualities of love (Gal. 6:22), self-control (Gal. 6:23), purity (1 Pet. 3:2), hard-work (Eph. 6:6–7), kindness (Gal. 6:22), and submission (Eph. 5:21) are attributes for which we all need to be striving. In the Titus 2 text we see these godly characteristics in relation to woman-to-woman discipleship. Whether we are a medical student, a shop assistant, or a retired missionary we can be effective members of the body of Christ by committing to informal or formal relationships in which we together seek to 'put on' this portrait of biblical femininity.

Why are we to do this? So 'the word of God may not be reviled' (v.5). These holiness-seeking friendships keep the Bible from being mocked by phony Christian living. In actual fact, Paul goes on to say that such godly living 'adorns' or 'beautifies' the doctrine of God (v.10). How amazing that we can adorn the doctrine of God in our biblical womanhood.

The Urgency

In some ways young unmarried women in today's world are in most need of this kind of input. They are perhaps not living in their parent's home and not yet protected and provided for by a loving Christian husband. The world's demand on them as they are out in the work place or on university campus leaves them thirsty for encouragement and training in purity and self-control. Regular contact with a female Christian mentor over a cup of coffee can powerfully counteract the pressure of living in Halls of Residence rife with sexual sin and wild definitions of womanhood.

Girls in their teens, still at home, can also benefit from support from godly student-aged women in their twenties. I remember from the church I grew up in, one girl who sung in the worship team used to frequently wear a short top that displayed a lot of her midriff. It was obviously immodest and distracting for some of the men in the 200 strong congregation. I was only a little older than her and I heard unhelpful comments made about it. Yet unfortunately her parents were not sensible enough to notice and no older woman took the responsibility to guide her in modesty. This is one small example of the great need of God-glorifying, bride-loving, Titus 2 relationships.

Titus 2—Practical

So Titus 2 speaks of an informal relationship that can be as practical as guidance on dress code.

One personal example of the huge practical benefits of older-woman younger-woman friendship is seen simply in my relationship with my mother. Frequently I ring and ask her 'homemaking' questions. Dad usually picks up and since I am in a rush (or more likely a fluster because something is burning on the hob) the conversation generally goes, 'hello Dad, sorry I have a "chicken question"', he chuckles and announces 'a chicken question' while passing the phone to my mum. Over the years, we've had all types of questions, from 'porridge questions' to 'plant questions'. Since I am not a great cook or botanist and my Mum has years more experience, I am grateful she can fulfil some of her biblical Titus 2 role in this way.

Titus 2—Word-Centred

Perhaps the most important mark of a Titus 2 relationship is the need for its conversations, rapport, and purpose to be fuelled by the Bible. A Titus 2 friendship is a feeding on the Word and its truth. For the cause of biblical womanhood in the United Kingdom today we need to hear young women revelling in their church friendships as the disciples did on the road to Emmaus, 'my heart burned within me while she talked with me and shared the Scriptures with me' (Luke 24). The Titus 2 mandate is not seeking out women who are spiritual giants but women who simply love the Word and want to open it up with others.

Savouring Christ Through Titus 2

So how can we savour Jesus? How can we enjoy our union with Christ? Our spirituality is shaped by our personal time and enjoyment of Christ but also by our community time and enjoyment of Christ's Bride. When we practically love, respect, obey, and serve the Bride of Christ, we love, respect, obey, and serve King Jesus. One way we practically revel in our oneness with Jesus is by pro-actively knitting ourselves to the Body to which we already belong. This means putting ourselves out in relationships: Perhaps being vulnerable, open and humble, and thinking about the good of Christ and his Bride and not ourselves. This makes us holy and strong by the power of Christ the Head. A biblical spirituality holds 'fast to the Head, from whom the whole body, nourished and knit together through its joints and ligaments, grows with a growth that is from God' (Col. 2:19).

Titus 2 is a biblical essential through which women of all ages and walks of life can savour their union with Jesus Christ. So speak to your women's worker, pastor's wife, or a godly woman in your church who can encourage you in this endeavour. Start praying, hunt down the younger women, show interest in them and get to know them, listen to their concerns, and let God use you. Perhaps as you've been reading this you have someone in mind. Savour your union with Jesus by savouring your union with your sisters in Christ.

Conclusion

Have you ever been a bridesmaid? Susan Hunt has said that Titus 2 friendships 'actually give us the privilege of getting the bride ready to meet the Bridegroom.' Being a bridesmaid can be a pretty daunting experience, however by my third time I was a little more confident in what I had to do; help prepare flowers, calm nerves, rearrange the veil, freshen up the make-up mid-day ...

When we serve the Bride of Christ by committing to the Titus 2 mandate it is the same honour as serving as a bridesmaid. And as in wedding etiquette it is the Bridegroom's duty to thank the Bridesmaids after the wedding feast, one day so too will Jesus Christ thank those of us who loved the Bride in this way. He will look at the beauty of his Bride and turn to us and say, 'Well done, good and faithful servant' (Matt. 25:21).

Discussion Questions

1. 'Living covenantally means that we are our brother's and sister's keeper. Women nurturing women is simply one way we live covenantally. It is as much a part of covenant life as gathering at the Lord's Table to remember Jesus' death until he comes again.' (Susan Hunt, 'Older Women Mentoring Younger Women,' in *Becoming God's True Women* (ed) Nancy Leigh DeMoss (Crossway, 2008), 161–170.)

Discuss this quote. What do you think it means?

2. Why do you think many of us don't commit ourselves to Titus 2 relationships? How can these concerns be resolved?

Crazy But True

10 | Savouring the Lord's Supper

I WRIGGLED on the squeaky faux leather pew and wished we were going home. Now the time had come in the evening service when everyone got deadly quiet and a little bit glum. Swinging my legs slightly, I stared at my mother. She looked very serious. She popped a tiny piece of white bread into her mouth and closed her eyes, retreating into a personal bubble. Then I watched the people around us do the same. It was all perfectly timed. Everyone was in unison. Take the bread, head bowed, eyes closed, and retreat. Only the minister's voice had the power to call these adults back to reality. I sighed again and wondered for the umpteenth time, 'what is Communion all about? And what is with the tiny glasses? I thought "supper" was soup and hot buttered toast?'

I knew the bread and the wine stood for Jesus' body and blood. I knew the Sunday School answers. This was a thing church people did to remember the cross. But I still did not really understand and this remained the case into adulthood. For years the Lord's Supper was just a twicea-month version of Remembrance Sunday with its two minute silence. Instead of those who died in the World Wars we remembered Jesus' death. Instead of fake red poppies we had fake red wine and small squares of bread. It wasn't until I started studying theology seriously that I came to realise that there is so much more to it than this. But at this point new questions began to plague me ... 'What is the correct way of taking the Lord's Supper?' and 'what is its spiritual significance?'

Biblical Help

I don't think I am alone. For many, the arrival of the bread and the communion cup generates confusion and uncertainty; not knowing what to do and how to take the bread and wine in a respectful and effective way. We don't want it to mean nothing but sometimes we don't know what it *should* mean. One clear solution is for us all to strengthen our biblical understanding of this amazing God-given grace. This chapter is dedicated to just this. As we set out a simple aid for developing a biblical appreciation of Communion we will see how it relates to our union with Christ.

This chapter is not a comprehensive answer to these questions—far from it. In the 'Recommended Reading' section of this book you will find books that open up the theology and practice of the Lord's Supper much further. I encourage you to check them out.

A Grace

This spiritual meal is called 'the Lord's Supper' because it was the Lord Jesus Christ who established it at the last supper he had with his disciples before he died. We read about this in the Gospel accounts:

> Now as they were eating, Jesus took bread, and after blessing it broke it and gave it to the disciples, and said, 'Take, eat; this is my body'. And he took a cup, and when he had given thanks he gave it to them, saying, 'Drink of it, all of you, for this is my blood of the covenant, which is poured out for many for the forgiveness of sins' (Matt. 26:26–28).

Jesus did this to celebrate and underline his complete and sufficient redemption wrought at Calvary. When he ripped open the loaf of bread he was drawing a big arrow to his body being ripped open on the cross. Then he gave it to his disciples to eat. The cup of wine similarly points to his blood running freely from his wounds, as he was literally 'poured out for many for the forgiveness of sins'. That too he gave to them to drink. The bread and the wine are signs and hallmarks of the forgiving power of Christ's body on the cross and the shedding of blood, for 'without the shedding of blood there is no forgiveness of sins' (Heb. 9:22. *cf.* Lev. 17:11). Yet we don't just look at the bread and wine, we eat them. We actively make them ours through digestion. By *physically* taking this meal we confirm our *spiritual* need for Christ. In our eating we declare our participation with Jesus in his death and resurrection. As he gave his disciples the bread and the wine, Jesus gives us himself on the cross. Praise God, he is ours.

The Lord's Supper, or the 'Eucharist' or 'Communion', is commonly called a 'sacrament'. This might be a term that sounds dusty, dull, and churchy. But one reason we use this word is to emphasise the grace behind this gift. This meal is a huge grace in our spirituality. Jesus gave it to us as a practical, visual, and spiritual means of growth in him. The more we treasure and appreciate the Lord's Supper the more we can savour Christ through it, anchoring our lives in gospel truth.

A Family Meal [1]

The Lord's Supper is also a meal that celebrates Christian unity by 'sharing together' in Christ. It is not merely a time of personal reflection briefly tagged onto the end of a service but a joyful family meal, in some way like the excitement we feel as we gather around for a special meal with our biological family. It is not only about the food but about each other. This is why Paul rebuked the Corinthian Church for not waiting for each other (1 Cor. 11:21, 33–34); it is a family meal. 'Because there is one bread, we who are many are one body, for we all partake of the one bread' (1 Cor. 10:17). This means that when we take the Lord's Supper, members of Christ's Bride should acknowledge one another, praying for one another and for family unity. Our hearts, minds and eyes should take in our brothers and sisters in Christ; the family of which we are a part, marvelling at the diversity and oneness in Christ. This moves us to grow in love, forgiveness, respect and commitment for the church family.

Maybe in the past you have not appreciated the Lord's Supper as a family meal? If we consciously enjoy the oneness we have with our brothers and sisters in Christ we will automatically lose any unhealthy tendency to retreat into a private bubble. Although the Lord's Supper is personal, when we come together with our church family, let us enjoy the glorious bride in her union with Christ.

A Helpful Acronym

Acronyms can be an effective method of reminding ourselves of correct teaching. In the past I have found the ACTS acronym (Adoration, Confession, Thanksgiving and Supplication) a useful way of checking that my prayer life is well-balanced and not just a shopping list.

In a similar way, I have found using an acronym to remind me of the Bible's teaching of the Lord's Supper a helpful check that I do not slip into confusion or over-familiarity. Importantly, this acronym is *not* a 'how to' guide or any such formula. And I don't necessarily mentally run through it every time I take Communion, otherwise this could be distracting. It is much simpler than that; learning the acronym has meant *learning and grasping the relevant Bible verses*. By this God's Word has renewed a passion and commitment in me for this Christ-feast. I hope you find the same.

E – examination

> 'Whoever, therefore, eats the bread or drinks the cup of the Lord in an unworthy manner will be guilty concerning the body and blood of the Lord. Let a person *examine* himself, then, and so eat of the bread and drink of the cup' (1 Cor. 11:27–29).

Here Paul is emphasising the need to properly discern Christ in the meal and not to partake just to satisfy one's physical hunger or thirst or merely a religious custom. Christ and his complete and sufficient salvation must be fully recognised. This means that only those who belong to Christ can have their part with him in this sacred meal.

In addition, the Christian has the holy duty to examine herself concerning unrecognised or ignored sin. Taking the time to fix our thoughts on the cross of Christ (using our God-given imaginations to see the humility, self-sacrifice, pain, and love) gives us an opportunity to see how vile our sin is. Here we can exercise our oneness with Jesus in his death and resurrection by engaging in some gutsy repentance of the filth that caused him to die naked on a tree. The person and work of the Spirit of Christ is our God-given assistance and guide in this. Therefore as we prepare to receive the bread and the wine we should ask the Father for the Holy Spirit to make areas of sin in our lives fully known to us, praying that his power and care will lead us to repentance and move us on in holiness. Whatever we need to confess and say sorry for we cannot truly grow in godliness if we offer God a superficial or vague repentance. Naming specific sins is a significant part of self-examination. Such prayerful participation in the Lord's Supper cultivates humility in us and stops us lazily dismissing sin. The Communion service is a time to stare ugly sin in the face, acknowledging how ugly it really is, and asking the cleansing Holy Spirit to help rid you of it.

M – memory

'Do this in *remembrance* of me' (1 Cor. 11:25).

This simple meal is for the sake of our memories. When we eat the bread and drink the wine it is to place Calvary firmly in our memories—to exercise our human minds for the glory of God and reorganise ourselves once again around the Cross. We are a visual culture and we have powerful imaginations that we can wield for our gospel good. When taking the Lord's Supper we can imagine Jesus nailed to the cross, the crowds shouting insults, our every sin being carried on his bleeding back, the thunder, the darkness, and the curtain torn from top to bottom.

At the same time, we are weak in our humanness and God knows this. God has been very gracious to give us this tangible 3D reminder of Calvary to help us after we have listened to a sermon. If our spiritual or physical senses have been dulled as we have sat sleepily on a Sunday evening, they can be awoken as we taste the bread and the wine; reminding us personally of Christ's powerful and gracious death and resurrection. We need to train ourselves to drum our hearts and minds at the Lord's Supper with the reality of our status as women buried and raised in Christ, saving us from a dungeon of sin and death, so that we can fully savour Christ.

P – proclamation

'For as often as you eat this bread and drink the cup, you *proclaim* the Lord's death until he comes' (1 Cor. 11:26). When the bride of Christ feasts together on his body, it is a public declaration to all creation of his victorious death. It is the redeemed, 'preaching Christ crucified' (1 Cor. 2:2) to the world. 2,000 years on from the cross, millions of Christians are still proclaiming the eternal victory of Calvary by this 'Christ-feast'. This unique and celebratory proclamation marks out the church from the rest of society.

This spiritual declaration is also a significant mark of belonging to Christ's bride, as she waits for the return of her bridegroom and head, Jesus Christ. We eat and drink 'until he comes' (v.26). The Lord's Supper is a feast of triumph and glory because King Jesus has defeated sin and death. Because he is victorious he is now sitting at the right hand of God (Luke 22:69). As we looked at in chapter four, because of this heaven is our home. So when we take the bread and the wine we can revel in our future glorious home with Jesus. We can get excited at the eternal inheritance that awaits us. On the day Jesus returns in power and splendour we will actually be there with him. This is the power of 'Christ in you, the hope of glory' (Col. 1:27).

T – thanksgiving

'... When he had given *thanks*, he broke it' (Luke 22:17, 19; C.f. Matt. 26:26–27; Mark 14:22–13; 1 Cor. 11:23–24). When Jesus gave thanks for the bread and wine he was essentially giving thanks to God the Father for his own flesh and blood. He is giving a prayer of thanks for his incarnation, his own God-man nature, and his coming saving death and resurrection. If you belong to Jesus and have been saved by the breaking of his body and the shedding of his blood on a brutal Roman cross, then thanksgiving to God is necessary for our growing in faith and love. Setting our spiritual eyes upon the infinite grace of the cross, symbolised in this meal, *can* move us to great wonder at the goodness of God and a profound sense of joy and praise for the person of Christ. We have to fight for this.

Y – yoked

'The cup of blessing that we bless, is it not a participation in the blood of Christ? The bread that we break, is it not a participation in the body of Christ?' (1 Cor. 10:16).

In feeding upon Jesus Christ we are yoked or joined to him by the Holy Spirit. This is our saving union with Christ, the truth we have looked at in this book which is central to the Christian life (John 15). Of this mystery, Bob Letham writes, 'True believers receive and feed upon Christ, as surely as they eat the outward elements. Christ is the key, for this is *the Lord's* Supper'.[2]

When we eat the bread and drink the wine, we are meditating *physically* (by taste and digestion), *mentally* (in thinking on the Word read and what we are doing), and *spiritually* (in our faith which the Holy Spirit uses to change us), on the fact that Christ is in us and we are in him. The physical act for the believer eating and drinking Christ's body and blood confirms that we have a share in him. He says this himself in John 6:56, 'whoever feeds on my flesh and drinks my blood abides in me, and I in him' (John 6:56). In this meal-of-grace our Lord and Saviour gives us himself by the power of the Holy Spirit. In giving us his body and blood he is strengthening and nourishing his bride. He is the husband in Ephesians 5:29 who cherishes his bride the church, self-sacrificially seeking her spiritual growth and maturity. Yet, distinct from any husband, he is both the means and the goal, for she feeds on him, the 'bread of life', so she can grow up in him (John 6:33, 35; Col. 2:19). The Lord's Supper is for our enjoyment of our in-Christ relationship. It can bring us Christian women great assurance and strength as the Holy Spirit works in us through it.

The cup is now EMPTY, as is the tomb! Jesus Christ is 'poured out for many' (Matt. 26:28). The work is complete—Hallelujah! In Christ, we are women who are connected, complete, and full in Christ!

Discussion Questions

1. As we have seen, the Lord's Supper is a time to say sorry to God for the sin and mess in our lives. J. I. Packer wrote, 'vague repentance is nothing, or at least next to nothing.'[3] What does he mean?

2. In what ways can the Lord's Supper feed our spiritual lives?

Conclusion | Wielding the Whole Armour of God

IF the gospel of Jesus Christ is going to make any difference in our daily lives, we need to wield it. We all muddle through the week's demands, distractions, and trials, at times giving little attention to the gospel that not only saves us but comforts and equips us. But our day can look very different if we have made our 'in-Christness' our worldview; allowing it to affect every little moment. As women in the Rock Jesus Christ we need to constantly remind ourselves of our true identity as daughters of the King, robed in the righteousness of Christ, heading for our heavenly home, and bought for holiness as a member of the Bride of Christ.

Where We Have Been
In this book we have rediscovered a spirituality based on the Bible's teaching of the Christian's oneness with Christ. We have pushed that stunning vintage armchair out from the back of the shop, dusted it down, polished it up, and set it in our living room. Now its full potential is realised as it is used daily and constantly admired.

We have seen that when we believe in Jesus we are fused to him by the power of the Holy Spirit. It is because of this supernatural connection to Jesus that we are saved and forgiven by his death and, by his resurrection, raised to a new life in him. This is why a Christian woman is a woman buried and raised in Christ.

We have also seen how this can change our lives in many different areas; how we view ourselves, how we deal with people, with the temptation to mess up, and how we respond to the world and the difficulties of life. As well as how it shapes our commitment to others in the church body, the Bride of Christ. How it moves us to love and support our sisters in Christ in Titus 2 relationships, and why we should treasure the family meal of the Lord's Supper as God's grace to us, for our enjoyment of the Lord Jesus and our maturity in him.

As we have dived into the subject of union with Christ we have come to see that this truth is not just about *knowing* the gospel but *living* and *enjoying* the gospel.

Where We End

As we draw to a close, we are going to reinforce in our minds the fact that our spirituality is about actively applying the cross of Christ every day. In the book of Ephesians, the Apostle Paul closes his letter to the church in Ephesus by giving them a fearsome encouragement to make them strong; he presents them with a suit of armour—the Whole Armour of God. We have talked about 'wielding' God-truth; to 'wield' is to handle a weapon with skill, 'to flaunt', 'swing', 'exert', 'employ' or 'command'. As we will see, as Paul names each item of armour he gives us a biblical example of 'flaunting' gospel truths in the face of temptation, for the sake of our enjoyment of King Jesus and the glory of God.

The Whole Armour of God

Hearing a long throaty growl behind her, Gemma spun round on her heel. Two piercing yellow eyes cut through the darkness and a fiery snort lit up her enemy's face. Gemma gripped her sword tighter and was comforted by the cool contours of the light-weight armour that clung like metallic skin to her chest and limbs. Squaring her shield across her body, she raised her blade; the double-edged Claymore catching the moonlight. Her adversary stretched out his neck and snarled at her. But Gemma stood firm; she was ready. The belt secured around her waist pulled Gemma's 5'5" stature up tall, and her pounding heart was well protected by her breastplate. The helmet, the shield, the shoes; every item she wore made her strong and courageous. The shadowy figure slowly crouched, preparing to attack. But he didn't have a chance. The battle had already been won by the King. Gemma smiled confidently, remembering his final victory and the mighty armour he had worn. She knew she would win. After all, the armour she was wearing ... was his.

Gospel Armour

A woman who has been buried and raised with Christ is in effect wearing his armour. Although she battles self, sin, and Satan, and at times, the world, she is fused to the victorious King by faith and in the power of the Holy

Spirit. This means his resources, found in the gospel, are at her disposal. We shall see what these resources are.

> Finally, be strong in the Lord and in the strength of his might. Put on the whole armour of God, that you may be able to stand the schemes of the devil. For we do not wrestle against flesh and blood, but against the rulers, against the authorities, against the cosmic powers over this present darkness, against the spiritual forces of evil in the heavenly places (Eph. 6:10–12).

Paul presents this armour to the Christians because of their oneness with Christ and for their strengthening. This is why he says, 'be strong *in* the Lord' (v.10). It is armour dependent on union with Christ. This means that if you are not a Christian you do not have it!

Paul tells us that this gospel defence is needed due to the fact that the material world is not all there is (v.12). There is a battle going on that we cannot see. It is a battle that belongs to God. He has already won it. But because the fighting against Satan continues, for now, God gives us his protection.

Forged by God

One of the most important things about the 'Whole Armour of God' is that it is the Armour of *God*. Paul may present the armour but it isn't his, it belongs to God. This means it is eternally strong, never to crack or shatter. It has been forged and crafted by divine genius, so it is a complete kit that meets all our needs. And it has been given to us generously by a loving and conquering King whose victory, strength, and power goes before us, for 'he disarmed the rulers and authorities and put them to open shame, by triumphing over them' (Col. 2:15).

Notice Paul doesn't finish his letter to the Ephesians with the words, 'now pick up any scraps of armour you can find!' That would hardly be an encouragement. But because *all* Christians (whether in second century Ephesus or twenty-first century U.K.), 'hidden with Christ in God', are given the King's Armour.

There is another vital part of the 'Whole Armour of God', and that is the word '*whole*'. Paul commissions his readers to put on or take up 'the *whole* armour of God' (v.11, 13). Just the helmet won't do. Your limbs and torso will be completely unprotected. Having every piece but the sword of the Spirit will leave you with no weapon and therefore defenceless. We can't be picky, we need every item.

Be Ready

Therefore take up the whole armour of God, that you may be able to withstand in the evil day, and having done all, to stand firm. Stand therefore, having fastened on the belt of truth, and having put on the breastplate of righteousness, and, as shoes for your feet, having put on the readiness given by the gospel of peace. In all circumstances take up the shield of faith, with which you can extinguish all the flaming darts of the evil one; and take the helmet of salvation, and the sword of the Spirit, which is the word of God, praying at all times in the Spirit, with all prayer and supplication (Eph. 6:13–18).

It is crucial that Paul uses phrases like 'be strong' (v.10), 'put on' (v.11, 14, 15), 'take up' (v.13, 16), 'fastened on' (v.14), 'stand' (v.11, 13, 14), and 'keep alert' (v.18). When we are given the Whole Armour of God we are expected to be active and responsible by clothing ourselves with it. The gospel is no good hanging up in our Christian wardrobe. In order to 'walk in Christ, rooted and built up in him' (Col. 2:6–7), we must fight for our allegiance to Christ and the killing of our sin. This means sometimes we have to engage the enemy when we meet him (although this doesn't mean going out looking for him). God has the power; it is his battle, his victory, and his armour. But we have to actively use it. Martyn Lloyd-Jones describes it as 'a perfect blending of [God's] power and my activity. It is my activity in and through the power that he gives me.'[1] As we related union with Christ to our lives, particularly in our identities, our sexuality, our relationships and in times of trial, we saw the need to be ready: To be sharp: To see sin and temptation coming.

Why does God give us this armour? That we 'may be able to stand against the schemes of the devil' (v.11), and 'withstand in the evil day' (v.13), by 'extinguish[ing] all the flaming darts of the evil one' (v.16). We need to be ready for Satan and his desire to pull Christians apart with guilt and shame. It is his plan to have us forget our union with Christ and spiral into a pit of sin. In 1 Peter chapter 5 Peter tells us to 'be watchful. Your adversary the devil prowls around like a roaring lion, seeking someone to devour' (v.8–9). Wearing the Whole Armour of God means we can 'resist the devil, and he will flee' from us (Jas 4:7).

What Is This Armour?

So we know the armour belongs to God. And that it is given to us because we are joined to Christ so we can stand strong in him against the evil purposes of the devil. But what is this armour?

- First Paul instructs us to 'stand therefore, having fastened on the belt of truth ...' (v.14). This belt, which is a pretty foundational piece of clothing that holds everything together, is the truth of the Word of God. Sometimes we find ourselves in a place of despair or unbelief. Trusting in the belt of truth can, like Gemma, bring our small humble stature up tall because we are trusting in the God of the Bible. We can stand firm and confident because we have fastened on the belt of truth of our union with Christ.

    There is more, in John 17:17 Jesus prays to the Father, 'sanctify them in the truth; your word is truth.' It is a simple formula; the more we know God's Word the more holy we are because the Holy Spirit uses the Bible to make us like Christ. This means with the belt of God's truth we are not just ready to fight, but being made a holy warrior as well.

- '... and having put on the breastplate of righteousness' (v.14), means securing tightly the truth that we are forgiven in Christ close to our hearts. When Satan brings guilt and shame down on us like a ton of bricks we can have the heart and mind assurance that 'there is therefore now no condemnation for those who are in Christ Jesus' (Rom. 8:1). A woman buried and raised with Christ adores the gospel and the purity of Jesus Christ because it covers her also and has rescued her from a pit, placing her clean and free on a palace roof.

- '... and, as shoes for your feet, having put on the readiness given by the gospel of peace' (v.15). These are no high-heels. Who can stand firm and alert in high-heels? One too many times have I had to remove an uncomfortable pair of high-heels and hobble around with blistered feet, open to the stones and dirt on the path. The readiness given by the gospel of peace is to be agile in the gospel, manoeuvrable, able to run, free from blisters and vulnerability because we are at peace with God through Christ. 'For he himself is our peace ... And he came and preached peace to you who were far off and peace to those who were near. For through him we both have access in one Spirit to the Father' (Eph. 2:14, 17–18).

- Paul also tells us 'in all circumstances [to] take up the shield of faith, with which you can extinguish all the flaming darts' of the devil (v.16). In this book we have seen the power of faith. It is our faith that the Holy Spirit uses to unite us to Christ. Faith is a powerful gift from God. Applying the reality of our spiritual connection with King Jesus to our daily situations is having faith in the gospel and holding it up, like a shield, when we are rained on with doubts, temptation, and the overwhelming complications of life. Satan can use anything to try and rob us of our enjoyment of Christ; our thoughts, our ministry, our lack of sleep, our hormones. But we can pull out the shield of faith with which God has lovingly equipped us. 'Under his wings you will find refuge; his faithfulness is a shield and buckler. You will not fear the terror of the night, nor the arrow that flies by day' (Ps. 91:5).

- Another important piece of this armour is 'the helmet of salvation' (v.17). The helmet of salvation is having a Calvary-centred mind. It is the clothing of our minds with the reality of the cross and knowing we are saved, forgiven, and adopted by Christ's blood. Paul draws attention to the mind because it is the first place we wrestle with sin. Either we fight the temptation and the thought disappears or we allow the thought to activate our will, and we act upon the sinful thought. If we fight sin in our minds we take 'every thought captive to Christ' (2 Cor. 10:5) and we glorify God by defending our minds with the truth of our salvation.

- As well as the helmet we are also told to take up 'the sword of the Spirit, which is the word of God' (v.17). Have you noticed that all the other pieces in the armour of God are defensive? The Sword of the Spirit, the Bible, is the only weapon we are given. The best example of the Bible being used powerfully as a sword is when Jesus wields it against Satan in the desert. In Matthew 4:1–11 we see Jesus standing ready, strong, and firm, almost spitting out the truth of the Word of God to his enemy.

Jesus really knows his Bible. Satan tempts him to use his power to make food but Jesus quotes from the book of Deuteronomy, 'It is written, "Man shall not live by bread alone, but by every word that comes from the mouth of God"' (Matt. 4:4. *cf.* Deut. 8:3). Next, Satan tries to coax him to use his power by jumping off the temple, but Jesus doesn't entertain this pointlessness and quotes Deuteronomy 6:16, 'You shall not put the Lord your God to the test.' Then Satan tries desperately to get Jesus to worship him, but he has had enough. Telling him to go away, he says, 'You shall worship the Lord your God and him only shall you serve' from Deuteronomy 6 verse 13.

Jesus knows the truth. He raises his sword and brandishes the Bible, and sin and Satan cannot touch him. We stand in his power, united to him. So we can do the same. They say 'every woman needs her handbag' but really every woman needs her sword. When we are in a haze of temptation and wanting to give in and sin, the best thing we can do is quote the Bible and walk off. So we need to eat, sleep, and breathe the Bible. Then we can say, 'I have stored up your word in my heart, that I might not sin against you' (Ps. 119:11).

Conclusion

I hope you have found this book helpful. We have seen the raw power of the gospel and our oneness with Christ, found in the Bible, and how it can save us for eternity whilst transforming our whole week.

Much of what we have looked at has demonstrated that the study of our Bibles and theology is vital. We need to understand Christian truth before we can live it out and wield it for our good and the glory of God. Unfortunately, some women see theology to be a 'man's thing'. This is not the case. Theology is for all believers. I personally encourage you to continue delving into the exciting treasure trove of theology, and do share what you learn with other brothers and sisters in Christ.

The gospel is all about Jesus. When we take hold of the forgiveness that Jesus Christ offers in his death, we are connected to him and safely hidden in him for life. The Bible gives us a spirituality of truth because Jesus is 'Truth' (John 14:6). And he is the 'Way' to a relationship with the whole Trinity; Father, Son, and Holy Spirit. It sounds crazy but it is true. One fourth-century theologian knew this so personally that he called the Trinity 'My Trinity'. Wow! In all our culture's search for spiritual peace and fulfilment, it is the beauty of Jesus Christ which is the answer: Our oneness with him, and with him only, brings us into an intimate relationship with the Holy and Awesome Trinity.

> *To know Him more I would aspire,*
> *To love Him with a heart of fire,*
> *Wrapped up in him, my one desire,*
> *Who first laid hold on me.*

FAITH COOK (b. 1937)

Discussion Questions

1. Read Ephesians 6:10–20 together and discuss why prayer is important to Paul's teaching here.

2. 1 Corinthians chapter 6 tells us we are 'washed', 'sanctified', and 'justified' in the name of the Lord Jesus Christ and by the Spirit of our God' (1 Cor. 6:11). What does this mean in relation to past sin?

3. Why not memorise the *Whole Amour of God* and use it as you pray for yourself and others.

Endnotes

Chapter 4:

1. 2 Sam. 17:3; Isa. 62:5; Jer. 2:2; Ezek. 16; Hos. 1–14; Matt. 9:15; John 3:29; Rev. 19:7; 21:2, 9; 22:17.

Chapter 7:

2. Edward Donnelly, *Life in Christ* (Bryntirion Press, 2007), 27.

Chapter 8:

3. Joshua Harris, *Stop Dating The Church: Fall in Love with the Family of God* (Oregon: Multnomah, 2004), 15.

4. Harris, 60–61.

Chapter 10:

5. An earlier version of this chapter appeared in *Evangelicals Now* July 2010, entitled 'The Lord's Supper: a helpful acronym to aid biblical understanding.' Used with Permission.

6. Robert Letham, *The Lord's Supper* (P & R Publishing, 2001), 46.

7. J. I. Packer, *A Passion for Holiness* (Nottingham: Crossway, 1992), 140.

Conclusion:

8. D. M. Lloyd-Jones, *The Christian Soldier: An Exposition of Ephesians 6:10 to 20* (Edinburgh: Banner of Truth, 1977) 54.

Acknowledgements

MY special thanks to Sheila Stephen and Dr D. Eryl Davies for encouraging me to write this book. Dr D, I am indebted to you for serving as my supervisor again, and self-sacrificially reading through pages written by a green writer.

Great thanks also goes to Angela Brand (mother of seven and grandmother of nineteen) and to Sarah Fuller for their kind corrections and wise comments. Appreciation must also be expressed to my parents (Nanny and Papa) for their babysitting service so that work could be done.

Thanks also goes to Rhona Black, my own Titus 2 friend and mentor; I love your friendship, your home, and your baking.

As always, it is my earthly hero and captain, Thomas, to whom I am most indebted. Your generosity in 'holding the fort' and sending me out to the University of Reading's snazzy library, particularly on your own study days, has been a stunning and revolutionary picture of the complementarian husband. Thank you so much!

Recommended Reading

Union with Christ:

Natalie Brand, *Complementarian Spirituality: Reformed Women and Union with Christ* (Wipf & Stock, 2013).

Edward Donnelly, *Life in Christ* (Bryntirion Press, 2007).

Elyse M. Fitzpatrick, *Found in Him* (Crossway, 2013).

Robert Letham, *Union with Christ: In Scripture, History, and Theology* (P & R Publishing, 2011).

Contemporary & Biblical Spirituality:

Wendy Horger Alsup, *Practical Theology for Women: How Knowing God Makes A Difference in Our Daily Lives* (Crossway, 2008).

Donald G. Bloesch, *Spirituality Old and New: Recovering Authentic Spiritual Life* (IVP, 2007).

The Lord's Supper:

Robert Letham, *The Lord's Supper* (P & R Publishing, 2001).

Eleanor Kreider, *Given For You: A Fresh Look at Communion* (IVP, 1998).